ASHEVILLE-BUNCOMBE TECHNICAL INSTITUTE

NORTH CAROLINA
STATE BOARD OF EDUCATION
DEPT. OF COMMUNITY COLLEGES
LIBRARIES

Y0-BCR-416

Discarded
Date MAR 2 5 2024

THE HIGHER
LEARNING
IN AMERICA:

A REASSESSMENT

Books by Paul Woodring

LET'S TALK SENSE ABOUT OUR SCHOOLS

A FOURTH OF A NATION

AMERICAN EDUCATION TODAY, with John Scanlon

NEW DIRECTIONS IN TEACHER EDUCATION

INTRODUCTION TO AMERICAN EDUCATION

THE HIGHER LEARNING IN AMERICA: A REASSESSMENT

THE HIGHER LEARNING IN AMERICA:

A REASSESSMENT

by Paul Woodring

McGRAW-HILL BOOK COMPANY

New York Toronto London Sydney

Copyright © 1968 by Paul Woodring. All
Rights Reserved. Printed in the United
States of America. No part of this publication
may be reproduced, stored in a retrieval system,
or transmitted, in any form or by any means,
electronic, mechanical, photocopying, recording,
or otherwise, without the prior written permission
of the publisher.

Library of Congress Catalog Card Number 68-16493
FIRST EDITION
71705

Acknowledgments

The author of a book with the title I have chosen must acknowledge his indebtedness to Thorstein Veblen, whose book *The Higher Learning in America* was published in 1918, and to Robert Maynard Hutchins, whose volume with the same title appeared in 1936. I am grateful to both of them not only for the title, to which I have added a subtitle, but also for the stimulus of their vigorous views and proposals—with some of which I have sharply disagreed.

This volume, which developed out of an address to the annual convention of the American Psychological Association on September 4, 1966, reflects some thirty years of experience with higher education as a teacher, administrator, writer, and foundation official. I am indebted to the Ford Foundation, its Fund for the Advancement of Education, and particularly to Alvin Eurich and Clarence Faust for the opportunity afforded me while I was a staff member to visit the campuses of many colleges and universities, to talk at length with presidents, deans, professors, and students, and to have time to think.

During my eight years as Education Editor and later Editor-at-Large of *Saturday Review* I have had occasion to read hundreds of manuscripts submitted for publication and to exchange correspondence with thousands of students, parents, faculty members, and other citizens, whose letters have helped make me more aware of the vast diversity of educational institutions in the nation. Many passages in the present book first appeared in *Saturday Review* in my editorials, articles, and book reviews. I am grateful to Norman Cousins and J. R. Cominsky for the oppor-

Acknowledgments

tunity to develop SR's Educational Supplement and to my editorial colleagues for their stimulating ideas.

Inevitably, my views of the higher learning in America have been greatly influenced by my personal experience in the seven colleges and universities with which I have been directly associated as student, instructor, professor, and guest professor, particularly Western Washington State College, which I have seen grow from a small teachers' college to a large state college that is now developing into a university and spawning a cluster of satellite colleges. My academic colleagues challenge all my views, while my students make me constantly aware of the rate at which the world is changing.

I am indebted to Ethel Church, amanuensis extraordinary, who typed the manuscript and corrected my spelling. And most of all to my wife, Jeannette, whose wise counsel based upon her own broad background of liberal education has broadened my perspective and helped temper my biases.

PAUL WOODRING

Contents

Introduction

The American people have an unbounded faith in education and tend to believe that if some is good more must be better. The view that education should be available to every child is firmly established. But two questions remain open: How many years of schooling should be required? And what proportion of our youth should be provided education beyond the minimal amount at public expense?

Before the Civil War, universal free public education meant only a few years of elementary schooling. It was assumed that once a child had been given the tools of literacy he would be able to forge ahead on his own, in school or out, and that any further education should be paid for by his parents. But the amount of schooling considered adequate has steadily grown over the last century as a result of urbanization, industrialization, automation, and the demand for trained manpower resulting from international threats and the adventure into space. Meanwhile, the nation's growing affluence has made more schooling possible.

During the last third of the nineteenth century the spread of public high schools across the land reflected a growing conviction that secondary education should also be free. The rapid growth of state colleges and universities gave indication of public awareness that the state's responsibility for education did not end with the secondary school. And during the first two-thirds of the twentieth century the demand for higher education increased so rapidly that the proportion of eighteen-year-olds entering college increased from 2 or 3 per cent to between 35 and 40 per cent while the number of college graduates in a single year increased from 27,410 to more than 500,000.

Today the rapidly growing number of community colleges with modest entrance standards seems to indicate that many Americans believe that at least two years of education beyond high school should be available to all who want it. But academic men have never been quite so certain that the higher learning is appropriate for large masses of people. While some educators have proposed that the liberal portion of higher education is appropriate for all free men, and others have insisted that college doors should be open to all who are intellectually qualified to profit from the higher learning, many have expressed doubts that more than a small percentage are, or can become, properly qualified. In the face of a rapidly growing population our most prestigious colleges, instead of expanding their facilities to meet the demand, have steadily raised their entrance standards, thereby seeming to reflect a conviction that higher education of a superior quality may properly be restricted to a select few.

These opinions reflect widely divergent points of view regarding the proper goals of the higher learning and of what a college or university ought to be. Thorstein Veblen, when he wrote *The Higher Learning in America* in 1918, defended the view that a university should accept responsibility for scientific and scholarly inquiry in pursuit of pure knowledge—and nothing else. His ideal university was not a place for the instruction of large numbers of young people. He saw no place in it for the training of students for such practical pursuits as medicine or law. He thought a few carefully selected students should be allowed to work closely with "the sages of the passing generation" but that the university should instruct no one except these future scholars. "Training for other purposes is necessarily of a different kind and is best done elsewhere," he said. "It does not become university work by calling it so and imposing its burden on the man and equipment whose only concern should be the Higher Learning." [1]

Veblen's ideal is approximated in some of our graduate schools, but it bears little resemblance to any total American university today. Instead of narrowing their scope, as Veblen proposed, universities have broadened their activities and have accepted many new responsibilities. His fight for a single-purpose institution, devoted exclusively to scholarly investigation, was a lost cause.

Robert Maynard Hutchins shares Veblen's doubts about the appropriateness of vocational and professional training in the university, but he sees much more clearly the need for broadly liberal general education at the undergraduate level. In his own volume, also titled *The Higher Learning in America,* published in 1936, Hutchins said:

> We can never get a university without general education. Unless students and professors (and particularly professors) have a common intellectual training, a university must remain a series of disparate schools and departments, united by nothing except the fact that they have the same president and board of trustees. Professors cannot talk to one another, not at least about anything important. They cannot hope to understand one another.
>
> We may take it for granted that we shall always have specialists; yet neither the world nor knowledge of it is arbitrarily divided up as universities are. Everybody cannot be a specialist in every field. He must therefore be cut off from every field but his own unless he has the same basic education that other specialists have. This means more than having the same language and the same general interest in advancing knowledge. It means having a common stock of fundamental ideas. This becomes more important as empirical science advances and accumulates more and more data. The specialist in a narrow field has all he can do to keep up with the latest discoveries in it. Other men, even in his own department, struggling to stay abreast of what is happening in their own segments of the subject, cannot hope to keep up in what is happening in his. They may now expect to have some general understanding of what he is doing because they all have something in common; they are in the same department. But the day will shortly be upon us when even this degree of comprehension will be impossible because of the infinite splitting of subject matters and the pro-

gressive submergence of any ideas by our insistence on information as the content of education.²

These words were both descriptive and prophetic. The "infinite splitting of subject matters" and the consequent spawning
of new departments has continued in response to the rapid accumulation of new data, particularly in the natural and behavioral
sciences. And, as the amount of raw data to be learned accumu-
lates, the "progressive submergence of ideas," particularly of the
kinds of ideas that transcend the individual disciplines, becomes
more apparent. Today there is even less communication among
professors in the various departments—even among those in the
same department—than there was thirty years ago. There is less
understanding of one another's problems and areas of knowledge
and less comprehension of the total reality for which the university is responsible. As a result there is less concern for the total
education of the student as an individual. The professor, particularly in the large universities, is apt to see each student as a potential future scholar in his own field rather than as a human being in
need of a balanced education. Such a view is compatible with
Veblen's view of the higher learning and he must be given some
measure of the credit or blame for it.

In most universities the typical professor does not care to talk
about the total education of undergraduates; even though he may
teach some of them every day he insists that he is not an educator—he is a chemist, physicist, mathematician, psychologist, historian, or a scholar in one of the other disciplines. He has only a
minor interest in the education of any students other than those
who wish to specialize in his own discipline.

In the smaller colleges that are not associated with universities
it is easier to find professors who feel a concern for the total education of students—that is why many of them have chosen to
stay in such colleges. But even here an increasing number of the
younger faculty members identify themselves with their disciplines rather than with the college or its students. In the graduate schools from which they received their Ph.D.s they were
heavily indoctrinated with the belief that universities are better

than colleges, that the teaching of graduate students is more honorific than the teaching of undergraduates, that the teaching of specialized subjects to seniors is more important than the teaching of interdisciplinary courses to freshmen, and that research is more important than any kind of teaching. Most young instructors, like most men in other fields, are status-seekers. They quickly discover that the status symbols of academia are rigged against good undergraduate teaching and that the way to get ahead in the academic world is to move to a university where one can spend most of his time in research. Or at least so it seems to the young men just out of graduate school. Only the more mature, and those relatively free of status-seeking propensities, are willing to remain in the small undergraduate colleges where good teaching is most respected, but where one has little opportunity to gain a national reputation.

Students are aware that something is wrong. To be sure, many enter college with no goal in mind but a well-paid job and are happy to enter upon their vocational training immediately, while others come only because they can think of no convenient alternative at the time. But the brightest students—those who are perceptive and intellectually curious—come to college eager to learn. They anticipate higher education as a great adventure. They come with many questions to ask and hope that their professors will help them find the answers. But they encounter professors interested only in a single subject who frequently are unable to understand the legitimacy of the questions because most of the big questions transcend the individual disciplines and consequently are not dealt with in graduate schools. This may explain why the colleges with the highest entrance standards are the seats of the greatest amount of student unrest, for it is the bright students who are not getting what they want during their undergraduate years.

In courses in psychology, sociology, anthropology, theology, literature, history, and biology, the student learns something about the nature of man. If he is bright he is aware that these must all be about the same man. But often his professors fail to say so and seem unaware of the interrelationships among the subjects.

Some of the problems that confront us result from a failure to distinguish clearly among the proper purposes of high schools, colleges, and universities. In their efforts to prepare students for admission to the institutions at the next higher level, high schools and colleges have lost integrity as unique institutions, each with its own identity and special purpose. In recent years they have raised their standards, with the result that students are working harder than ever before, but all too often their way of raising standards has been to emulate the higher institutions—colleges have become more like graduate schools while high schools have taken on some of the less desirable features of the college.

Hutchins foresaw the danger of this a third of a century ago when he said: "The most striking fact about the higher learning in America is the confusion that besets it. This confusion begins in the high school and continues to the loftiest levels of the University. The high school cannot make up its mind whether it is preparing students for life or for college. The junior college is in most places an extension of the high school curriculum, which is there applied to an essentially similar though somewhat smaller student body. Here also the question of whether the students are completing their education or are preparing to go to the university has not been settled, and the aims of the institution are not clear. . . . The college of liberal arts is partly high school, partly university, partly general, partly special. Frequently it looks like a teacher-training institution. Frequently it looks like nothing at all. The degree it offers seems to certify that the student has passed an uneventful period without violating any local, state or federal law and that he has a fair, if temporary, recollection of what his teachers have said to him . . . little pretense is made that many of the things said to him are of much importance." [3]

Today it may be that a greater number of the graduates have violated some of the local laws and they have also gained a temporary recollection of a greater number of facts. But the confusion about the purposes of the institutions has grown with the years. So have the numbers—today the number of students enrolled in colleges and universities is twelve times what it was when Veblen was putting his thoughts on paper and four times what it was when Hutchins wrote his book on the higher learning.

Veblen is no longer with us to comment on the changes of recent decades, but Hutchins' judgment seems to be that the quality of higher education has not improved over the years. Speaking in 1964 to the Association of American Colleges he said of our institutions of higher learning: "Their standards are undecipherable, their accomplishments dubious, their pretensions insufferable, their independence a sham, and their appeal to their constituents irrational and degrading."

Both Veblen and Hutchins are strong-minded individuals who express their views bluntly. Because of this, and because both define the purposes of education more rigorously and more narrowly than has been customary with American educators, their books have led to endless controversy. Because both were perceptive and informed insiders, their views could not be ignored. But since their books were written the higher learning in our nation has changed dramatically. It is time for a reassessment.

THE HIGHER LEARNING IN AMERICA:

A REASSESSMENT

PART ONE
THE HALLS OF LEARNING

1. A Confusion of Institutions

Throughout the history of the United States, higher education has dwelt in a state of happy anarchy. Anyone with the necessary funds—an individual, a private group, a religious body, or a unit of government—has been able to establish a college or, if it preferred, a "university." Each institution has been free to establish its own entrance standards, decide for itself what kind of a faculty it wished to recruit, make its own curriculum, and invent its own degrees. Except for those that have been incorporated into the recently developed state systems of public higher education, and with the possible further exception of those in New York where even nonpublic colleges are responsible to the State Board of Regents, this freedom exists even today despite the best efforts of the accrediting agencies to establish minimal standards. As a result, the responsibility for the higher learning in the United States now rests with a vast and confusing array of separate and diverse institutions: colleges, institutes, professional schools, junior colleges, universities, and multiversities, each with its own history, traditions, and goals.

Our lack of centralized control is a natural consequence of the desire on the part of those who established the Republic to protect states' rights. The word *education* does not appear in the United States Constitution. Though some of the Founding Fathers, notably Jefferson, Washington, and Franklin, were convinced that a free nation could not flourish without an educated citizenry, those who wrote the Constitution chose to leave to the separate states the responsibility for providing schooling. As a result we have no national system of education, no national

3

university, and no cabinet officer or other federal official to whom all schools and colleges are accountable. The U.S. Office of Education in the Department of Health, Education, and Welfare, though it has a growing responsibility for the disbursement of federal funds, has no direct control over educational institutions, students, faculties, or standards.

American higher education grew upon the base of the nine colleges founded in the colonies before the Revolution: Harvard, William and Mary, Yale, Princeton, Dartmouth, Brown, King's (which became Columbia University), Rutgers, and Franklin's Academy (which became the University of Pennsylvania). All of these except Franklin's Academy were originally church-related, but they have gradually loosened their religious ties.

Since the Revolution, three kinds of institutions, independent, church-related, and state-supported, have developed side by side. During the first half of the nineteenth century many religious groups established colleges, or schools optimistically called colleges, to advance learning, promote the faith, and prepare ministers. A few colleges independent of either church or state control were founded during the same period.

In most parts of the nation, state colleges are as old as the non-public ones. The published founding dates for both public and private colleges must be examined skeptically because they often refer back to the establishment of a secondary school out of which the higher institution developed much later, but it seems clear that Georgia, North Carolina, and Vermont established universities, or colleges or academies destined to become universities, before 1800. Other states, including South Carolina, Ohio, Michigan, Virginia, and Wisconsin took the step before 1850. The development of state-supported higher institutions was accelerated by an act signed by President Lincoln in 1861 that provided grants of land to assist the states in founding colleges, and by 1900 every state had a state university, a land-grant college, or both.

In the twentieth century fewer church-related colleges have

been founded than in the nineteenth. Higher standards have increased the costs of starting a college to a point where they exceed the financial resources of most denominations. But many municipal institutions, including junior and community colleges, have been founded since 1900, and nearly 200 state normal schools have evolved into colleges or universities. And, though the various kinds of institutions serve somewhat different purposes, the competition among them for both funds and students has been a frequently troublesome aspect of American higher education.

Of all our colleges and universities, only a few loom large on the national scale. Obscurity is the common fate, partly because there are so many of them. A high school graduate, at the time he selects his alma mater, is not likely to know even the names of more than 10 per cent of the institutions that offer him an opportunity for further education. Asked to make a list, he probably will start with Harvard, Yale, and Princeton, but unless he lives in the East he is not likely to recall the names of all the other five members of the Ivy League. He has heard of Notre Dame, of course, and of perhaps thirty other universities whose names are prominent on the sports pages. If he is academically oriented he may be able to name twenty-five or thirty institutions noted for their graduate and professional schools. He may recall the names of a few small colleges which have attracted nation-wide publicity in one way or another. These same institutions—fifty to one hundred at most—are known to almost everyone and consequently are named as first choice by a much larger number of students than they have room for. It is this fact that gives rise to the false impression that our colleges have room for only a small proportion of the students desiring higher education.

In addition to these brand-name institutions, the student is aware of a few additional colleges that happen to be near his home or in which his friends or relatives have been enrolled. He can vaguely recall the names of still others but is probably uncertain whether the State University of New York, the University of the State of New York, and New York University are the same or different institutions. He may confuse the University of Washington with any of several others named for the first president. He will be puzzled by the many St. John's, the two Miamis, and the four Northwesterns. If he tries to pad out his list by naming the fifty states, and assuming that each must have a university, he will get many of the names tangled. There is, to be sure, a University of Michigan, one of Illinois, and of Minnesota but there is no University of Ohio though there is an Ohio State University as well as an Ohio University. When he has completed his list the student probably will make his selection while still unaware of the existence of 90 per cent of the colleges in the nation—one of which might well have been a better choice for him than any of those to which he applied.

The student can hardly be blamed for his ignorance because no one can be familiar with all the institutions of higher learning in the United States. No one is sure how many of them exist—at any rate there is no agreement among those who do the counting. The statistics are hopelessly confused, both by uncertainty about which should be classified as "higher" and by doubt as to what should be called an "institution."

The most widely quoted figures are those of the U.S. Office of Education which lists some 2200 separate institutions, of which 1500 offer courses leading to the baccalaureate or higher degrees. The others are junior colleges which in 1967 were increasing at the rate of about one per week. But other estimates range from 1200 to 4000 or more. Gene Hawes in his *Guide to Colleges* [4] gives detailed information regarding 3658 individual institutions all of which are "higher" in the sense that they enroll only students who have completed twelve years of elementary and secondary schooling. The larger numbers include unaccredited schools, Bible schools, business colleges, and other vocational schools offering short courses. But a part of the confusion about numbers results from the varying degrees of independence and individual identity enjoyed by the various colleges and campuses.

The University of California, for example, though it is governed by a single Board of Regents, is located on nine campuses hundreds of miles apart, each of which has its own chancellor, faculty, and student body. Should it be counted as one institution or nine? And, if it is nine, should each of the various named "cluster colleges" on the Santa Cruz campus also be counted as separate institutions?

Should Hunter, Brooklyn, and the other colleges that have now been combined into the City University of New York be counted as separate institutions? And how shall we list the many campuses of the State University of New York, many of which were separate colleges long before the University was established? Perhaps such questions are of interest only to statisticians, but the conflicting answers given to them help explain the confusion about numbers. It seems obvious that, within our complex establishment of higher education, the term *separate institution* has no clear meaning.

The distinction between colleges and universities is not much clearer. Universities are usually larger and more complex, but San Francisco State, which enrolls 18,000 students and offers 67 different types of bachelor's degrees and 40 different master's degrees, is called a college, while Kansas Wesleyan, which enrolls 600 students and grants only the A.B. degree, is called a university. For reasons that have been lost in history, some religious denominations were particularly prone to apply the university label to every little college they founded. For reasons that are contemporary, and include competition with universities already established in the same states, some state colleges are prohibited from changing their names to university, however large and complex they become.

Names give no clue to quality, prestige, or selectivity. Of the thirty institutions listed by Cass and Birnbaum in their *Comparative Guide to American Colleges* [5] as "most selective" (a term that means "hardest to get into" rather than "best") fifteen are either universities or colleges within universities, three are institutes, while twelve are content to call themselves colleges.

The distinctions among institutions classified as public, private, independent, church-related, and denominational are rarely sharp and clear. In the West it is safe to say that Stanford is a private university and that Berkeley is a campus of a public one, even though Berkeley has a large private endowment while Stanford is not at all reluctant to dip into the federal treasury. But in Pennsylvania such "private" institutions as Temple, the University of Pittsburgh, and the University of Pennsylvania receive major portions of their income from the taxpayers of the state. Rutgers, which started out in the eighteenth century as a private college, became New Jersey's land-grant college in 1864 and is now the State University of New Jersey. Cornell, though in part a private university, is also the land-grant college of the state of New York.

The U.S. Office of Education lists some 700 institutions as denominational and 400 as independent. But other sources list more than 800 as church-related. The difference is accounted for by the fact that many of the colleges established by religious bodies have gradually loosened their ties with the churches. Most of those founded by Congregationalists have long been free of church control. In 1967 several Catholic institutions, among them Notre Dame, the University of Portland, and St. Louis University, announced their intention of inviting laymen, including non-Catholics, to become members of their governing boards. It seems probable that many more of the denominational colleges will soon become independent of church control. The possibility that independence may soon make them eligible for more federal grants provides an additional inducement.

Though coeducation is the general rule in American colleges and universities, there are numerous exceptions. Of the 2200 higher institutions listed by the U.S.O.E. 260 admit only women and 255 only men, but most of these are small private colleges that all together account for no more than 6 or 7 per cent of the total college population. Virginia is the only state university to exclude women, and it has adopted Mary Washington as a coordinate college, but several of the state colleges in the South admit only one sex. Today Harvard men and Radcliffe women sit side by side in classes, take the same examinations, and receive the same diplomas. In 1967 Yale extended an invitation to Vassar to move from Poughkeepsie to New Haven (which Vassar later declined) and rumors were afloat that Princeton was looking for a women's college with which to affiliate. It seems that most college girls now want to be "where the boys are" and the boys do not object. Consequently it is doubtful that many colleges for one sex only will survive the present century. This would come as a surprise to our ancestors. Prior to the establishment of Oberlin in 1833 as a coeducational college, no college in the United States admitted women, and for many years after that fears were still expressed that coeducation would lead to moral disaster. Perhaps it has, but no one seems to mind very much.

Our various institutions of higher learning have grown at vastly different rates. Today they range in size from colleges with fewer than 100 students to university systems enrolling more than 100,000. Some are close-knit communities of teachers and students while others are little more than administrative offices for campuses scattered all across a state.

Except for a few in the South, American colleges are open to members of all races, and nearly all, even those supported by churches, admit students of all faiths. But in other respects the diversity is as great as the range in size and complexity. Some boast of their placid rural settings while others stress the advantages of their urban surroundings. Some take pride in the ivy that obscures their ancient buildings while others boast of glossy structures much too new for ivy. Some house all their students in dormitories, others have encouraged fraternities or sororities to provide housing, while still others are day schools that cater to commuters. Some boast of professors who are great teachers while others prefer faculty members who are pious and well-behaved; but the majority take the greatest pride in professors who are productive scholars, and some boast of the number who have won the Nobel Prize. About the only thing that all have in common is the fact that they require a high school diploma or its equivalent for admission.

Considering the lack of centralized control, it seems remarkable that there is as much uniformity as now exists. Some practices have become fairly well standardized as a result of tradition, emulation of older colleges by the newer ones, and the work of voluntary accreditation agencies. Among our institutions there is quite properly a great diversity of goals and, not quite so properly, a wide range of standards for the same degrees.

Efforts to centralize control on the state level seem to have created as many problems as they have solved. Because students are not interchangeable units, education does not readily lend itself to mass production. As the system grows, the multiplying echelons of administrative authority increasingly separate the individual learner from those who make policy regarding his education. Bureaucracy takes over and opportunities for individual initiative and the acceptance of new ideas are reduced. There is doubt that the efficiency is increased or that money is saved. In any case, independent and church-related colleges are not at all eager to be incorporated into statewide systems.

The present confusion of institutions, though it seems disorderly to Europeans and indefensible to many Americans, is not likely to be eliminated very quickly. It corresponds too closely with our concepts of democracy, freedom, individual initiative, and local self-determination, and is a part of what Frederick Lewis Allen once called "the Unsystematic American System" which, for all its defects, has some virtues all its own. It helps preserve the dignity of the human individual. And it offers assurance that any dictator who tries to get control of higher education in the United States will have a hard time.

2. The Elm-shaded Campus

For two and a half centuries after the founding of Harvard in 1636, the dominant institution of higher learning in North America was the liberal arts college—often a small church-related institution in a rural setting. "Going to college" meant four years on an elm-shaded campus in ivy-covered buildings, far from the temptations of city life. Most of the colleges were boarding schools which accepted responsibility for the student's social, recreational, and religious life as well as for his academic education. Such colleges had no counterpart in Continental Europe, where liberal education was the responsibility of secondary schools and where most of the universities were urban institutions, committed to the advancement of scholarly learning and to the training of men for the learned professions.

Harvard was modeled after one of the colleges at Cambridge, where colleges were housing and tutorial units, part of a university which administered examinations and granted degrees. But in New England, because there was no university to which Harvard could attach itself, the college found it necessary to offer all its own instruction and to become a degree-granting institution. Thus was born the American liberal arts college. Other American colleges modeled themselves after Harvard.

Although nearly all American colleges and universities now offer the liberal arts degree, the term *liberal arts college* usually refers to a small independent or church-related college not associated with a university. Hundreds of such colleges were founded during the early nineteenth century in all parts of the country. Though many kept the cost of instruction low by staffing their

faculties with retired ministers and with missionaries who had returned from foreign lands, many were so poorly supported that
they did not survive. Those that did survive were not always
highly regarded by academic scholars, particularly scholars
steeped in the German tradition. Veblen, who identified the
higher learning with universities, spoke contemptuously of
small, church-related, undergraduate colleges, calling them "a
precarious class of schools . . . such as are content to save their
souls and to remain alive without exerting any effect on the current civilization [and] are able to get along with faculties made
up exclusively of God-fearing men." [6] But these colleges were
held in much higher regard by most Americans. They provided
the major part of the higher education in this country until
the universities and state colleges began to grow late in the century.

The proportion of students attending independent and church-
related liberal arts colleges has declined steadily for a century,
and continues to decline. Those within the group that have resisted the urge to expand their offerings and become universities
now enroll no more than 15 to 20 per cent of all the college students in the nation. They have also suffered a relative decline in
prestige and attractiveness to young people of college age—a decline obscured by the vast amount of favorable publicity given to
a few small colleges of superior reputation. Some forty or fifty of
these colleges—the "prestige" institutions—are nationally known
and highly respected in the academic world. These are colleges
that have chosen to remain small, have focused their attention on
liberal education, and have resisted the demands for undergraduate vocational courses and for the establishment of graduate
and professional programs. They have assured themselves of talented graduates by admitting only talented freshmen. Their increased visibility has enabled them to attract funds from foundations and private donors, and the growing number of candidates
for admission has enabled them to raise their tuition fees. This in
turn has enabled them to pay the salaries necessary to attract superior faculties.

Though the future of such colleges is secure, it would be difficult to name 100 that come close to fitting such a description.
What of the others—perhaps 700 of them? While some belong in
the "obscure but good" category and others are adequate though
undistinguished, the sad fact is that many others, including some
fully accredited colleges with long histories, are less than adequate by today's standards. Some are struggling to stay alive, and
for perhaps 200 or 300 the prospects for survival are not bright.

Part of the trouble is financial. The sources of income and endowment on which their stronger and more prestigious rivals
depend are not available to these weaker institutions. Foundation
money goes most often to colleges that already have strong faculties and highly select student bodies. Colleges that have made
their contribution by educating ministers, teachers, and housewives have few rich alumni. Campaigns urging everyone to
"Give to the college of your choice" do not produce much revenue for obscure colleges that few have chosen. And a large part
of the federal money for higher education goes for research and
consequently is not available to small undergraduate colleges. The
total effect of the combined efforts of foundations, government,
industry, and fund drives has been to make rich colleges richer
while the poor ones remain poor. And the poverty of many private colleges—at least 200 to 300 of them—is appalling.

The tragic state of their finances is revealed in faculty salaries.
In the mid-sixties the median salary paid to faculty members of
all ranks in nonpublic colleges with enrollments of fewer than
1000 was less than $7000. Some of those in the lowest quartile
paid salaries in the $4000-to-$5000 range. Yet most of these are
fully accredited colleges that grant the liberal arts degree; some
of them bear famous names and have a long history.

In the past these colleges have been able to hold some competent teachers despite the low pay. The authors of a study made
for the American Council on Education in 1966 [7] conclude that
"even the weakest, humblest, struggling college seems always to
have a nucleus of able, dedicated teachers who will stay with the
institution through times of adversity as well as prosperity. These

are persons who could, if they wished, move to better positions but who, for reasons that are not always clear, choose to stay where they are. . . . Sometimes it is religious conviction that holds them, often it is loyalty to the kind of education and the kind of relationship with students that is possible in the small liberal arts college."

But while this has been true in the past it seems unlikely that it will be true in the future. The younger faculty members, themselves the graduates of specialized graduate schools, do not feel the same loyalty to undergraduate liberal education as did the older generation of teachers. They are finding that it is just as easy to become dedicated to a professorship that pays $12,000 or $18,000 as to one that pays $6000. They are moving on to state colleges, to universities, and to positions in industry and government.

The deterioration of the faculty is not the only problem faced by a poorly financed college. Prospective students who visit the campus find the decaying buildings, the libraries, and the laboratories inferior to those in the high schools they have attended and draw their own conclusions. As a result, the weakest of the nation's private colleges find it difficult to attract students even in this period of bulging enrollments. In the eighties, when the declining birth rate begins to affect the colleges, they will find it impossible.

In their efforts to survive, the weaker colleges have made questionable claims and have resorted to futile tactics. Some have insisted that educational quality is unrelated to faculty salaries. Many have claimed too much for the hallowed tradition, the intimate environment, and the low student–teacher ratio. Some, while boasting of their freedom from political control, have abjectly accepted the equally stultifying controls of provincialism and parochialism. While condemning state colleges as godless they have themselves substituted piety for learning. Some, while retaining the name of liberal arts colleges, have transformed themselves into low-grade vocational schools. In an effort to attract students, some have expanded their lists of course offerings without expanding their faculties or facilities.

Such tactics are futile. The best chance for the survival of the small private college lies in doing what it can do best—offering a first-rate undergraduate education of a truly liberal but not highly specialized nature. A college with little endowment and no outside support cannot hope to provide first-rate professional training of any kind. Without expensive laboratories and shops it cannot train technicians and specialized scientists. But it can teach well the humanities, the social and behavioral sciences, mathematics and the natural sciences. And it can keep the love of learning alive in students who will later go on to universities for their specialized study. But it can do these things only if it has a competent faculty. One inspiring professor does more to build up a college than two or three second-raters, and in the present market first-rate college teachers cannot be had for salaries in the $6000-to-$7000 range.

While even a very small college can offer sound introductory instruction in the major disciplines at the freshman and sophomore levels, it dilutes its efforts if it attempts to provide major areas of concentration in all the academic disciplines. It is not necessary that it do so. While the larger undergraduate colleges offer majors in thirty to thirty-five subject areas, a small college might be wise to concentrate on the four or five areas in which its faculty is best qualified. If it is located near other colleges it can arrange some sort of consortium whereby students desiring majors not available in their own schools can take some of their work from another college with an exchange of credit. Such a plan would make it unnecessary for each college to attempt to cover all the areas of knowledge at the upper division level. I shall discuss other alternatives in my final chapter.

Whatever steps are taken, it seems certain that the nonpublic small college will never again play the major role it played in the early nineteenth century. But it can provide educational opportunities for many students; it can experiment with new approaches to learning; and it can continue to contribute to the diversity of higher education in America.

3. Universities, American Style

Though the meaning of the word *university* has changed with the centuries and differs from one country to another, a university is never just a large college. It has additional purposes that are discharged by a number of more or less separate schools, colleges, or faculties. Traditionally a university prepares young men—only recently women—for the learned professions and also accepts responsibility for the advancement of learning through the discovery of new knowledge. Those in England offer instruction beginning at about the level of that in our undergraduate colleges, but most of those on the Continent do not. It is assumed that students have acquired an adequate background of general liberal education in the secondary schools, which are more advanced than our American high schools. Students from the German *gymnasium* and the French *lycée* are admitted directly into the graduate and professional programs of Continental universities. American higher education borrowed some elements of the English tradition in the seventeenth and eighteenth centuries and others from the German tradition in the nineteenth, and we have attempted to combine them in a not altogether compatible marriage. We have also added features not found abroad, particularly the emphasis on public service.

The universities that appeared during the Middle Ages at Bologna, Salerno, Salamanca, Paris, Naples, Padua, Genoa, Oxford, and Cambridge were the chief centers of intellectual inquiry in the newly emerging Western culture. In the centuries that followed, their influence declined, or at any rate they lost some of the characteristics of universities. William Selden says:

"In an era of enlightenment influenced by such men as Descartes and Hobbes, Newton and Leibnitz, Voltaire and Diderot as well as Montesquieu and Adam Smith, the learned world was identified with society, not with educational institutions. The universities went their peaceful way, catering to the young men of birth and breeding, concentrating attention not on new learning but merely on the preservation of the old." [8]

In the New World, colonial universities were established in Mexico in 1554 and in several of the South American colonies during the same century. But in the United States, where liberal arts colleges catering to young men of birth and breeding preceded the founding of the Republic, the university is a much newer institution. Though a number of colleges optimistically used the label during the early part of the nineteenth century, and though Yale granted the first earned Ph.D. in 1861, Johns Hopkins (founded in 1876) has some basis for its claim to being the first true university in this country. Modeled after the German universities, which had achieved a high level of excellence in that century, "The Hopkins" was something new in the United States. From the beginning it emphasized research and offered programs leading to the Ph.D. degree. For a time it accepted no undergraduates. It came close to being the kind of institution Veblen thought a university should be.

During the next quarter of a century, Harvard, Yale, Columbia, and a number of other American institutions changed themselves from colleges with attached professional schools to true universities. Clark was established as a university in 1887 and enrolled no undergraduates until 1902. Stanford had many of the characteristics of a university as well as the name from the time it was founded in 1885. In 1892 William Rainey Harper, with the help of $35 million donated by John D. Rockefeller, established Chicago as one of the nation's foremost universites.

State institutions, many of which had been called universities from the time they were founded, also moved toward true university status between 1880 and 1910. In 1900, when the Association of American Universities was formed, those considered worthy of membership included three state-supported institutions—California, Michigan, and Wisconsin—and eleven nonpublic ones. But the next nine to be admitted, between 1900 and 1917, were all state universities: Virginia, Illinois, Minnesota, Missouri, Kansas, Nebraska, Indiana, Iowa, and Ohio State.

Between 1861 and 1900 the number of academic doctorates (mostly Ph.D.s) conferred annually rose from one to 382. Today it stands at about 18,000 and is expected to rise to 37,000 by 1976. These figures give some indication of the expansion of graduate education.

All the emerging universities emphasized research and preferred professors who were "productive scholars." Now, for the first time, professors were called upon to teach both graduate students and undergraduates and to conduct research and write for the learned journals, all at the same time. This was the beginning of the "publish or perish" controversy—more accurately called the conflict between teaching and research—of which we have not heard the last. The problem was more acute on this side of the Atlantic than it had been in Europe, where university professors are rarely called upon to teach undergraduates.

Universities compete vigorously for funds, status, professors who are productive scholars, and students who are highly motivated and academically talented. Some of the sharpest competitive struggles are between the public and nonpublic institutions. Between 1850 and 1900 the private colleges bitterly resisted the efforts of state institutions to become universities, insisting that they should be technical schools only and leave the higher learning to nonpublic institutions. More recently the denominational colleges have fought against allowing state colleges to offer liberal education. Today the competition is more covert—public statements stress the need for cooperation—but it still is not unusual for state institutions to be condemned from the pulpit as godless. And in the state legislatures private-school forces still work quietly behind the scenes to prevent the expansion of tax-supported higher institutions.

One's view of the relative merits of state and private universities depends on where he lives. Harvard and Yale loom much larger than any of the state universities in New England. But who can name a private university in the state that rivals the University of Michigan or one in Wisconsin that can be compared to the University of Wisconsin? In California, Stanford competes with the State University, and in Illinois, Chicago can at least challenge the public university at Urbana; but in neither case is the private institution clearly superior, whatever its alumni may believe. In Oregon, Washington, Minnesota, Iowa, Colorado, or Arizona, it would be difficult to name a nonpublic university that offers much of a threat to the state universities in those states.

In New England and the Middle Atlantic states, the colonial colleges that eventually became universities had become prestigious before anyone thought of establishing state universities. Harvard predates the University of Massachusetts by 237 years. Columbia grew out of King's College, founded in 1754, while the State University of New York did not come into existence until 1948. Where the state institutions were late arrivals they found it necessary to take what was left of both students and faculty members after the private schools had their pick. For a long time they were poorly supported by state legislators, many of whom were private-school graduates who doubted that higher education was a proper responsibility of the state. Only after 1945, when it became apparent that the private colleges could not provide for the tidal wave of students, did the northeastern states begin to provide adequate assistance for the support of public higher education. Now the state universities, particularly those of Massachusetts, Connecticut, and New York, are rapidly moving ahead; but it will take time for them to catch up with either the private colleges or the state universities farther west.

West of the Alleghenies, public and private institutions of higher education came into existence at about the same time. Ohio University at Athens was established in 1804, Oberlin in 1833, Western Reserve, in Cleveland, in 1826, and Miami in 1809. The University of Illinois, founded in 1867, is twenty-four years older than Chicago but sixteen years younger than Northwestern.

The University of California predates Stanford by twenty-two years. Several of the western states with smaller populations—Arizona, Nevada, and Wyoming—still have no private universities though each has at least one state university.

Students living in the West are much less likely than those in the East to believe that private schools offer a better education than that which is available in state universities. Consequently the state universities of the West get their full share of the brightest students. And, because they can outbid most of the private schools nearby, the state universities of the western states get more than their share of the most able faculty members. Though the big state universities have suffered from their public image as "football schools," it is doubtful that over the years they have emphasized muscular activities any more than such private institutions as Notre Dame, Southern California, NYU, Pittsburgh, Texas Christian, or Southern Methodist. And though most of them got their start as land-grant institutions offering instruction in agriculture, they are rapidly losing their "cow college" reputation. Today most of their students would not know a Jersey from a Holstein. They draw their students from all social strata, with the largest number coming from the middle class because most Americans belong to that class. They are the alma maters of about half the men and women in the U.S. Senate today and of the governors of about half the states.

Most of the state universities maintain excellent professional and technical schools and many of their graduate schools rank high. In an assessment of quality in graduate education conducted by the American Council on Education in 1966 (an assessment based on professional opinion of relative quality) the Berkeley campus of the University of California ranked along with Harvard while the graduate schools of the universities of Michigan, Illinois, and Wisconsin compared favorably with those of Yale, Columbia, Princeton, Stanford, and Chicago.

Liberal education is something else again—something in which the state universities, with a few exceptions, can take less pride. Though each institution maintains a "College of Arts and Sciences," headed by a dean, and grants the A.B. degree, few maintain a corps of teachers that can properly be described as a liberal arts faculty. Students pursuing the A.B. degree select from among the specialized courses taught by members of the graduate and professional faculties or, more often, by graduate teaching assistants who are paid a modest fee for teaching freshmen and sophomores while they themselves pursue their doctorates. Such assistants are not necessarily poor teachers; most of them are bright and scholarly, and some teach very well. But by and large their loyalty is not to liberal education.

The professors who teach undergraduate courses in state universities rarely meet to discuss the problems of liberal education—they do not really function as a liberal arts faculty. Curriculum-making is left to the dean or to a small committee in which each member battles for his own discipline rather than for the interests of the student.

Admission standards differ widely among the state universities. Michigan, Wisconsin, Connecticut, Massachusetts, Vermont, New Hampshire, and perhaps two or three others can be classed as very selective or highly selective. California requires a B average in high school. But most of the state universities will admit any student with a C or C-plus average in high school, and some are required by state law to admit any graduate of an accredited high school in the state. But low entrance standards do not necessarily mean low standards for graduation. The universities with the lowest entrance standards have also the highest attrition rates—some drop from 30 to 50 per cent or more of their students during the freshman and sophomore years for failure to make satisfactory grades. This ruthless weeding-out policy seems to be more acceptable to state legislatures and the public than a rigorous admissions policy. On the whole it is doubtful that private universities can be said to have higher standards, either for entrance or for graduation, than public ones. They must be judged as individual institutions rather than on the basis of their source of support.

Whether it is public or private, the American university in the second half of the twentieth century appears to be a thriving institution. Well-qualified students by the tens of thousands are competing for admission. Graduates, including those with advanced degrees, are in great demand. Professors, deans, and presidents are eagerly sought as consultants to industry and government. Library and laboratory facilities are expanding rapidly as millions of dollars are poured into the treasuries by foundations and the federal government as well as by alumni and students. If the university were a commercial enterprise it would be classified as a growth industry.

But a university is not an industry. Rapid growth based on a greater demand for its product only complicates its problems. During the period of greatest expansion, communication is breaking down on many campuses, students and faculty are in revolt, and fear is growing that the institution is becoming all but ungovernable.

Speaking at Princeton in the fall of 1965, President James A. Perkins of Cornell commented: "The modern university is one of those strange paradoxes of human affairs, dangerously close to becoming the victim of its own success. At a time when there is the greatest clamor among students for admission to the university there is the greatest dissatisfaction with the conditions of student life and studies. . . . At a time when research is richly supported—and respected—it is being described as the academic Trojan horse whose personnel have all but captured the city of the intellect. And at a time when faculty members are in greatest demand for service around the world, there are intimations that their efforts to save the world will cost us our university soul." [9]

The wide range of judgments of the success of American universities results from the fact that different observers focus their attention on different aspects of the universities' work. Those who judge their quality as research institutes find them highly successful—a substantial portion of the world's best research now is conducted under the auspices of American universities. Those who judge them by the products of their professional schools usually find them partially successful, though they identify many flaws. Those who are concerned with the liberal education of young men and women often conclude that American universities, with a few exceptions, are failures. Some have suggested that they ought to give up trying to educate undergraduates and should leave liberal education to the separate colleges, which take it more seriously.

Adlai Stevenson once said in an address: "Men are born free; they cannot be born wise, and it is the duty of the university to make the free wise. . . ." Unfortunately, few American universities accept such a duty. But unless the student gains some measure of wisdom as well as knowledge and professional and research skills, he does not become liberally educated. He learns to make a living but not to live wisely.

4. The New State Colleges

Most of the state institutions that once were land-grant colleges have become universities—in name if not always in fact. Today's state colleges—some 200 of them located in forty-five states—have a different history. With a few exceptions they got their start in the nineteenth century as normal schools established for the purpose of preparing teachers for the elementary schools. During the first half of the twentieth century—in most cases during the twenties and thirties—they undertook the education of secondary as well as elementary teachers and became four-year degree-granting teachers' colleges. More recently they have added liberal arts programs leading to the master's degree, and they have dropped *teachers* or *of education* from their names. While some have become universities and others have been absorbed into state university systems, thereby losing their separate identity, a substantial number of them, particularly in the western states, are evolving into institutions of a new kind—one that for want of a better name is called the general state college to distinguish it from the state university, the single-purpose teachers' college, or the community college.

Though they enjoy various degrees of local prestige, even the best of the state colleges are not well known outside their immediate localities. They do not boast the unique features that attract nationwide attention to Bennington, Antioch, or other experimental colleges. Their football teams do not achieve the success that made sports fans elsewhere aware of Notre Dame. They lack the reputation for exclusiveness that attracts status-seekers, and their names do not appear on anyone's list of prestige colleges.

Yet these unheralded institutions are already the alma maters of several million Americans, one of whom is President of the United States. And, except for the junior colleges, they are the most rapidly growing institutions of higher education in the nation. Already they enroll at least a million students—the eighteen in California alone enroll nearly 200,000. They are destined to play a much larger role in the future than they have in the past.

The range of quality in state colleges—even of those within a single state—is as great as that in private colleges; some are excellent, some are mediocre, some deserve their obscurity. But, in contrast to the denominational colleges which are severely handicapped by lack of funds, the quality of state colleges is improving almost everywhere. In the East—particularly in New England, where they are overshadowed by famous private colleges—they, like the state universities, had a long struggle to gain adequate state support. Even in the 1950s some were so poorly equipped and lacking in prestige that they were unable to attract more than 200 or 300 students even at a time when other colleges were overcrowded. But in other parts of the nation, where private colleges are fewer and less distinguished, state colleges are thriving institutions with magnificent new plants, well-equipped laboratories and libraries, and competent faculties. Several of those in California have enrollments of 15,000 to 20,000 even though they restrict admissions to the upper third of high school graduates. The average salaries of state-college faculties are below those of major universities but above those of private colleges; consequently the state colleges are now in a position to seduce professors away from all but the most affluent private undergraduate colleges.

One reason that even the strongest state colleges are not well known in other parts of the country is that they have little need for nationwide publicity and consequently seek it less avidly than do private colleges. They are not dependent on donations from individuals, corporations, or foundations. Except for a few in the East, they have no difficulty attracting students. They know they will survive and prosper so long as state legislatures make the necessary appropriations for capital outlay and operating expenses. Nationwide publicity would attract more students from outside the state, and this might make legislators less willing to provide the funds that keep tuition low. A reputation for exclusiveness would have the same effect.

Another reason for their obscurity is the cumbersome names inflicted on these colleges by state legislatures. A rollcall sounds like a Boy Scout boxing the compass: Northern Michigan, Northeast Louisiana, Eastern Kentucky, Southeast Missouri, Southern Oregon, Southwest Texas, Western Washington, and Northwestern State. The names of twelve American colleges start with *Western* and eight more start with *Southwestern*. No matter how excellent a college may be, it is not likely to gain a national reputation if no one can remember its name or distinguish it from other institutions with similar names. If Harvard had been named Eastern Massachusetts College of Arts, Sciences, Medicine, and Law it would never have been able to compete with Yale and Princeton.

Whatever the reason, state colleges get a bad press—when they are mentioned at all they are treated patronizingly by Eastern writers and editors. *Newsweek*, in its issue of December 30, 1963, said of President Johnson's alma mater: "Southwest Texas State—unpretentious, old-fashioned, square and upright—mirrors Johnson's own personality." Southwest Texas State is probably no more old-fashioned or square—or for the matter more upright—than any of the hundreds of independent and church-related colleges in towns of comparable size. It is true, however, that state colleges reflect both the faults and the virtues of middle-class America and, except for the few located in large cities, of towns and small cities rather than of metropolitan society. Few of the students come from farms, however, because few Americans now live on farms.

Most state college students come from families with modest incomes: not those considered modest by a Madison Avenue executive, but incomes considered modest by a schoolteacher, minister, or small businessman. Many of them are of the first generation in their families to enter college. Parents who are themselves college graduates, particularly those in the upper income brackets, are more likely to send their offspring to a private college or a large state university because they remember the day when the state college was a normal school and they still think of it as such. But the great majority of state college students are not sent to college by their parents or anyone else. They go of their own volition, sometimes against their parents' wishes, and often at their own expense. A large majority work part time during the school year and full time during the summers. As a result, though they may lack social sophistication, they develop the kind of maturity that comes to those who make their own decisions and pay their own way.

Even when they were called teachers' colleges, these institutions enrolled many students who did not intend to become teachers but chose the college because it offered higher education at a cost they could afford. Most of them charge little or none of the tuition cost to the students. Fees assessed to students are rarely more than $200 to $400 per year. But since many of the state colleges are located in smaller cities and towns—those in San Francisco and Los Angeles are exceptions to the rule—most of the students live in dormitories. Living costs have risen sharply, with the result that state colleges are no longer the "poor man's colleges." That distinction has fallen to the community colleges and metropolitan institutions that cater to commuters.

The students who enter state colleges today have much in common with those who enter middle-grade private colleges. They have survived the same teen-age culture, and their view of life has been molded by the same motion pictures and magazines. Many have attended the same high schools, where they were athletes, valedictorians, student body presidents, cheer leaders, drum majorettes, and editors of school newspapers.

But unlike students in Ivy League colleges, where 30 to 50 per cent of the freshmen come from independent preparatory schools, nearly all state college students are graduates of public high schools. And unlike those in colleges with highly selective entrance requirements, state college students represent a wide range of academic talent.

Whether this diversity is a handicap to the bright and well-motivated student is anybody's guess. Some educators believe that the bright student will not come up to his potential level of achievement unless he is isolated, during his college years, from those of more limited talents. But others are just as firmly convinced that a bright student is more likely to develop his talent for leadership if he can associate with members of a more heterogeneous group.

The faculties of state colleges are made up of a more complex mixture of personalities and points of view than is found in most private colleges—a mixture that results from the rapid changes these colleges have undergone. In many of them the transition from normal school to teachers' college to comprehensive state college has taken place within the memory of older members of the faculty. The make-up of their faculties reflects their history.

In most of the state colleges there are still some professors who joined the faculty when the institution was a normal school or teachers' college. Normal schools recruited many of their teachers directly from the public schools and rarely required them to hold doctoral degrees. These schools placed great emphasis on good teaching, but they assigned teaching loads much too heavy to allow time for research or scholarly writing. Consequently some of the senior professors in each state college lack doctoral degrees and few of them have distinguished records of scholarly publication.

Younger faculty members, brought in to teach the expanding list of academic courses, come from a different tradition; they have been recruited directly from the academic divisions of graduate schools. Most of them are indistinguishable from those who join the faculties of private colleges and universities; they have the same scholarly outlook, the same high standards, the same preferences for narrow specialization. Unfortunately, many of them also have the same attitudes toward teacher education—ranging from indifference to contempt.

Such attitudes reflect the fact that the American people, and particularly those within the academic community, have never been willing to take teacher education seriously or to believe that a college devoted to it can compare in quality with one that educates dentists, accountants, farmers, housewives, or Wall Street brokers. An exploration of the reason for this, in a nation that stresses the value of education, would make a good topic for a doctoral dissertation in social psychology. But a fact it is: colleges that educate teachers have never been able to gain much prestige as institutions of higher learning. It is partly for this reason that the younger faculty members in state colleges have been eager to drop *teachers* or *of education* from their names.

The younger instructors and assistant professors are eager to remake their institutions. Because they were indoctrinated in graduate school with the view that every professor should be a productive scholar, they are not willing to accept the leadership of older faculty members who do not hold a Ph.D. and have not published. But the older professors who have devoted many years to their institutions are not eager to surrender control of the college to the Young Turks.

The schism between the younger men, dedicated to their own disciplines, and the older ones, dedicated to teaching, presents a difficult problem for state-college administrators. But the attrition that comes with time will take care of that. The great danger is that when the younger men take over, the college will acquire some of the worst traits of a second-rate university. But a few of the more fortunate state colleges have found professors and administrators who combine the best of the two traditions: men of scholarly outlook and background who are in sympathy with the state-college tradition and willing to build upon it. These institutions will become the leaders.

Though it must raise standards and accept new responsibilities, the state college cannot turn its back on teacher education. In a nation with 50 million boys and girls of school age, this would be disastrous. At least 25 or 30 per cent of our college graduates are needed as teachers and because private colleges produce fewer than their share the state institutions must provide more.

But a sound program of teacher education is in no way incompatible with high intellectual standards and a strong liberal arts emphasis. There is now widespread agreement among educators that the proper education of teachers includes a judicious blend of liberal education, scholarly knowledge of the subject to be taught, and professional training. There is a growing conviction, too, that the major emphasis must be liberal—that liberal education is not the antithesis of teacher education but its heart.

The notion that teacher education is an inferior form of higher education, and that it consists primarily of professional training, can no longer be tolerated in any college. And the notion that educating teachers is less important or less academically respectable than educating members of other professions must be rejected completely by professors of all departments. It will be ironic if the colleges that give their greatest attention to teacher education—institutions scorned in the past for their neglect of liberal education—become the ones that accept the responsibility for preserving the liberal arts tradition when that tradition has died in the so-called liberal arts colleges. And it may well happen.

It is certain, however, that the state colleges of the future will accept many obligations in addition to that of educating teachers; already the number of students planning to teach has dropped to fewer than half in many of these colleges. Already they have lost their identity as single-purpose institutions. What, then, should they strive to become? They cannot safely emulate other institutions with different traditions and purposes. They should not become pale imitations of great universities or expanded versions of the small private colleges. They need the imagination and courage to build themselves into new and different institutions.

Population pressures and the greater demand for college education, coupled with the fact that private colleges are not in a position to accept their share of the growing number of students, make it certain that state colleges will continue to grow rapidly. They will no doubt continue to expand their list of offerings. But the growth and the program expansion will be most rapid in those states that are least adequately supplied with strong private colleges.

But what of educational quality? Differences in leadership, in quality of faculty, in tradition, and in willingness of governing boards to support higher standards make it certain that by 1980 the differences among state colleges will be even greater than they are today. Some will settle for mediocrity; they will be content to accept students rejected by more distinguished institutions and will offer a modest form of higher education for students of limited aspirations. But those that have a clear sense of purpose and a vision of what they might become will transform themselves into distinctive institutions with high standards and traditions of excellence. They will attract first-rate students and distinguished faculty members. And they will not remain obscure.

5. Colleges for Commuters

Though reliable figures are hard to come by, it seems a safe esti-
mate that half the students enrolled in American higher institutions today live at home during their college years. The half who
commute includes most of those enrolled in junior colleges,
community colleges, municipal universities and university extension centers, a substantial proportion of those attending private
universities located in large cities such as NYU, the University of
Southern California, Temple, and the University of Pittsburgh,
plus a smaller but significant proportion of those enrolled in those
state colleges and universities located in urban centers. Some are
part-time students who work part of the day and attend late-
afternoon or evening classes, but many are students who carry a
full academic load but who live at home because it is convenient,
because it is believed to be less expensive, or because their parents
are reluctant to have them leave home.

About half of the commuters—roughly a million and a half
students—attend two-year institutions traditionally called junior
colleges but increasingly, particularly in the case of publicly supported ones, called community colleges. Of more than 700 two-
year colleges in the nation, about 100 are independent, more than
100 are church-related, and more than 500 are publicly supported. But the public institutions, being on the average much
larger than the private ones, enroll the great majority of the students.

Junior colleges came into existence early in this century; Joliet,
established in 1901, is usually given credit for being the first. But
the greatest expansion of publicly supported two-year colleges

has occurred since the end of World War II. California now leads the list with seventy-five, followed by New York with thirty-four and Texas with thirty-two. But these figures will soon be outmoded because new ones are being established at a rate of about fifty each year.

Some of the public junior colleges are supported by local communities and governed by local school boards; others have their own boards, while some are supported in large part by the state and are under the control of statewide boards which make policy for all the junior colleges in the state.

Public two-year colleges usually charge no part of the tuition cost to the student and hence, for students living at home, are considered the least expensive of all institutions of higher education. Most of them have no entrance requirements except a high school diploma. Typically they offer three kinds of program: courses for students who plan after one or two years to transfer to a four-year college or university, terminal courses of a general nature for students who do not plan to go on to another institution, and vocational courses of a wide variety.

Because of their low entrance standards, the public junior colleges usually enroll a large proportion of students who made only average or below-average grades in high school and who do not score high on college entrance examinations. But, particularly among the students planning to transfer, there is a substantial minority of students of high academic potential who choose the junior colleges for financial reasons. These make good records in the four-year institutions to which they transfer.

Many of the teachers in two-year public colleges are recruited from among the local high school teachers, but some come directly from the graduate schools. Compared to university professors, they are likely to be more interested in teaching and less interested in research; consequently they are, in many cases, excellent teachers for freshmen and sophomores taking courses that are not highly specialized. The salaries of teachers in public junior colleges are higher than those in small denominational four-year colleges and only a little below those of teachers in four-year state colleges. Often the salary scale is the same as that used in the local elementary and secondary schools; but because the junior college teachers have more advanced degrees, their salaries are more often at or near the top of the scale that in some school systems now goes up to $10,000 or $12,000 and in nearly all systems goes up to at least $8000 or $9000, which is above the median salary in small nonpublic colleges.

The commuter colleges have made higher education possible for many students to whom it might otherwise have been denied and have thereby contributed to the upward mobility of many Americans. Not only do these colleges offer the full range of subjects provided by residential colleges, but on the average the quality of instruction is probably as good. A student who lives at home while in college can study all the liberal disciplines and can prepare himself for any profession or other vocation that requires a college education.

But even when the instruction is excellent, the student who lives at home misses a great deal of the traditional college experience. Traditionally, going to college has meant leaving home and making a sharp break not only from family life but from the community in which the student grew up. It has meant an end to close parental supervision. While in college the student lived in a dormitory, a boardinghouse, or a fraternity or sorority house, in which he learned that there are other ways of life and other kinds of people than those he knew at home. In a residential college he associated with other young people from many parts of the country and from other lands. His intellectual and social horizons were broadened; he lost some of his provincialism.

The commuter is much less likely than the residential student to take full advantage of the social, recreational, and cultural features of college life. He finds it difficult to get back to the college library in the evening and does not have the opportunity to take part in the late-evening bull sessions characteristic of dormitory life. Many commuting students have complained that their parents continue to hover over them and to treat them as children, and some report that their mothers establish hours for them to do their "homework." Childish habits are hard to break when the student continues to live in his childhood environment. Living at home the student finds it difficult to develop an adult attitude toward learning or toward life.

If the college enrolls a large proportion of commuters, as many community colleges do, or if it enrolls only residents of the city, as was true until recently of the city colleges of New York, the dangers of provincialism are obvious. According to one report, nine-tenths of the students at Brooklyn College have never lived outside the city of New York and half of them have never traveled beyond its immediate environs.[10] A student who meets throughout his college years only other residents of his own community is almost certain to remain provincial in outlook even though the community is a large city. Even his accent is likely to remain intact. The student who leaves college each day immediately after his last class is also unlikely to form close friendships with his classmates or to develop a feeling of identity with his college. He is more likely to continue to associate with those he knew in high school and to identify with his home community rather than with the larger world.

In the case of the student who works part time while in college, these disadvantages are partially offset by the fact that the alternation of work and study is, in itself, educationally valuable. Colleges such as Antioch, which draw most of their students from an economic class in which young people do not find it necessary to work, make much of the educational values of work-study plans that are organized by college officials. Less affluent students, who are forced to work at paying jobs to support themselves while in college, have always been able to get such experiences without having them planned by the college, with the result that they have become more resourceful and self-reliant. But the fact that a student is employed while in college does not make it essential that he continue to live at home.

Is it really necessary for so many students to live at home during their college years? The reasons usually given are economic. But much of the saving may be illusory. The cost of tuition, fees, books, and clothing is the same whether a student lives at home or away from home. The commuter—unless he lives in New York and travels by subway—usually must have a car. Even if he buys a jalopy, the cost of the car and gasoline would pay his room rent in a dormitory for a long time—typical room rent in a dormitory is rarely more than two to three hundred dollars a year.

Living at home reduces the cost of food somewhat, but food costs money even when it is eaten at the family table; and commuting students usually buy at least one meal a day at the college. Is the saving in food cost sufficient to justify letting a student spend many hours in transit during his college years—hours that might more profitably be spent studying? It seems entirely possible that if students looked carefully at the relative costs of living at home and living near the college—and if they also gave consideration to the relative value and completeness of the kinds of education gained in each case—the number of commuters would be much smaller than it is now.

Though the commuting students miss much of the college experience and probably save less money than they think, it seems certain that their numbers will continue to grow. Most of the colleges founded in the past two decades have been located in urban centers and have been especially designed to attract commuting students. When new state colleges are planned, state legislators argue vehemently that they must be located in or near the fastest-growing centers of population.

If college is to mean more than just going to classes for three hours a day, special provisions must be made for the social and recreational activities of commuters and for their intellectual stimulation outside class. Some urban colleges have substantially reduced the disadvantages of commuting by providing browsing rooms, meeting rooms, music rooms, hobby shops, comfortable places for study and conversation, and recreational facilities in order to keep the students on campus for more hours of the day and to encourage them to become more identified emotionally and intellectually with the institution of higher learning.

The provincialism characteristic of student bodies made up entirely of students from a single city can be partially offset by encouraging the enrollment of some students from other parts of the country and from foreign lands. This is well worth while even if it necessitates the building of a few dormitories for such students. A program of college exchanges would also be beneficial in enabling the student to spend at least one of his college years in another part of the country. For a boy or girl who has never been outside New York City, a year in California, Iowa, or Tennessee might be more broadening than a year in Europe—and almost as sharp a contrast. The student from Iowa would be equally enriched by a year in New York, San Francisco, or Boston.

6.   Prestige, Selectivity and Educational Quality

The Academic Totem Pole

When Stanley Woodward, sportswriter for the New York *Herald Tribune*, gave the Ivy League its name in the 1930s he did not intend it to become a symbol of excellence or academic purity. He pointed out that some varieties of ivy are poisonous and others are frequently potted. But those associated with the league ignored his warning. A few years later a Columbia alumnus, who may or may not have had his tongue in cheek, wrote a blast in a national magazine declaring the schools in that league to be vastly superior to all other colleges which he referred to as "the outer mediocrity." He described state universities as "educational rabbit warrens." And many readers believed every word of it.

During the 1950s *Ivy* took on a special éclat that extended to dress as well as to education. Frederick Birmingham, in his entertaining and informative book, *The Ivy League Today*, says that during that decade " 'Ivy Fashion' became an absolute uniform among the college students of the nation. It was also adopted by nightclub comics, prizefighters, delivery boys, and gangsters appearing before Senate committees. . . ." [11] Though the uniform has now become less popular, the prestige of Ivy still captures the imagination of the young and of their ambitious parents.

Though Ivy Leaguers have come to believe their own mythology and have had a considerable amount of success in convincing

38

both students and parents that *Ivy* means all that is best in higher education, the fact is that the Ivy League is not an educational organization. It is an athletic association made up of eight undergraduate men's colleges that have little in common except their location in the northeast corner of the United States. Though most of them are relatively old as American colleges go, all are very young by European standards. One was founded in 1865—more recently than many of the state universities in the Middle West. One is an independent college while the others are parts of universities. One is a part of a land-grant university complete with such non-Ivy appurtenances as cowbarns and pigpens. Since few Americans living west of the Alleghenies can even name all the eight members of the League it seems clear that the others bask in the reflected glory of Harvard, Yale, and Princeton, which are the names everyone associates with Ivy.

But the tragic fact remains that to many status-seeking Eastern students, failure to be admitted to an Ivy League college seems a fate worse than death. Some are so embittered that they are unable to adapt themselves to the other colleges that eventually do accept them or to profit from what those colleges have to offer.

Though some high school students are apparently unaware of the fact, educational quality is not the exclusive possession of a single athletic league; nor, for that matter, is prestige. Such schools as Antioch, Bennington, and Sarah Lawrence have gained a special kind of éclat from the widespread publicity given their experimental approaches to higher education. Though most of their innovations are now decades old and hence no longer experimental, the prestige lingers on. Swarthmore, Carleton, Oberlin, Reed, and perhaps twenty-five or thirty other small colleges have gained high prestige, particularly among academics, from the fact that their graduates do well in graduate school.

Prestige differs from one part of the nation to another. Nicholas von Hoffman, in *The Multiversity*, observes that *Eastern* and *Western* as applied to colleges and universities are not geographic regions but concepts of what a college or university ought to be.[12] "There are Eastern schools in the West such as Berkeley, Reed, Oberlin, Antioch, Chicago, and possibly the University of Michigan," he says. It has been my observation, too, that the schools he mentions are most highly respected by people living in New York and New England, presumably because they conform to the Easterner's concept of education with its exclusiveness and high entrance standards. Asked to name the best college in the Pacific Northwest, most knowledgeable Easterners will say "Reed" without hesitation. It is probably the only one they ever heard of. But if you ask the man on the street in Portland the same question, he is likely to name a state institution and to add that Reed is a curious place inhabited by students who are eager to go barefoot and wear beards. And Hoffman might have added that there are some "Western" schools in the East. The University of Massachusetts and the University of Connecticut resemble the land-grant universities farther west and hence find it difficult to acquire prestige among New Englanders even though they are improving rapidly in quality.

The Berkeley campus of the University of California has achieved nationwide publicity from two divergent distinctions. It has come to be known as the focus of student unrest. It has also been acclaimed as having one of the nation's top graduate schools. It may be no accident that a university rated so high for its graduate program should have trouble with its undergraduates. It seems reasonable to suppose that, in building up its graduate school as a research institute, Berkeley has neglected its undergraduates—that while eagerly attracting Nobel Prize winners to its faculty it has failed to attract the kind of teachers undergraduates need. At any rate this is among the charges made by Berkeley undergraduates.

Why, one might ask, has Harvard, which also has a high-ranking graduate school, not had similar student uprisings? There is, of course, some discontent among Harvard undergraduates, but much less than at Berkeley. The answer may be partly a matter of climate—not the fog of San Francisco Bay but the particular social climate of the Bay area—but there is another reason.

When an alumnus says with pride "I am a Harvard man" (and they do manage to work it into the conversation), he means that his degree is from Harvard College, which has a long tradition dating from 1636. But Harvard University is a much newer institution. A graduate or professional degree from the University does not really make one a "Harvard man."

A Berkeley alumnus does not take similar pride in his college because, as an undergraduate, he scarcely knew he was in a college. He saw himself as a minor cog in the vast machine that is the Multiversity of California. Such identification is not conducive to high morale except for those who are proud of the football team. Consequently the Berkeley student feels that he has little to lose if he takes action that is harmful to his alma mater.

The student who selects a college on the basis of its prestige runs a considerable risk. The prestige of an institution of higher learning does not always rub off on its students and graduates. Some alumni of Ivy League colleges remain totally obscure throughout their lives, while some graduates of unheard-of universities become famous. The statistical differences among the graduates of the two kinds of institution give little comfort to the individual who chooses a prestigious one and yet never amounts to much after graduation.

Selection on the basis of prestige can also be a mistake if it is assumed that prestige is a guarantee of educational quality. No doubt the two traits are positively correlated, but the correlation is far from perfect, both because prestige may result from extraneous factors such as the social class of the students admitted and because there is a time lag between a rise and fall in educational quality and a rise and fall in prestige. A college's position on the prestige totem pole often tells more about the kind of institution it was a generation or two ago than about its present educational quality.

Selective, More Selective, Most Selective

The colleges once called exclusive were those that preferred students of impeccable ancestry and sometimes denied admission to members of minority groups. Such colleges are now rare; the trend of recent years has been away from such aristocratic bases for selectivity and toward the Jeffersonian view that educational opportunity should be based upon individual capacity. Selectivity has replaced exclusiveness as a basis for institutional pride. Today even the most prestigious colleges are willing to ignore a student's ancestry if he gives sufficient evidence of academic capacity. Though this trend is consistent with democratic principles it still leaves some complex problems unsolved because it is difficult to measure an individual's potential apart from the opportunities he has had as a result of his economic and social background.

A selective college, as the term is used today, is one that chooses its students on the basis of secondary school grades and scores on college entrance examinations. These criteria are used because they have been found to correlate positively (though far from perfectly) with college grades. The selective colleges make the rather dubious assumption that those who make high grades are the ones who profit most from college and hence are most deserving of higher education.

It should surprise no one that high grades in high school are predictive of high grades in college. Though the exceptions are too numerous to be ignored, in general grade-getters continue to be grade-getters. Nor is it surprising that students who make high scores in entrance examinations make high grades in college classes where grades are based in large part on more examinations. But no one can seriously believe that grades are the proper goal of higher education. And the assumption that those who make high grades are the ones who profit most from their education and are most likely to make the greatest contribution to society after graduation should be re-examined, for it must withstand a considerable amount of contradictory evidence.

When critics point out that neither Churchill nor Roosevelt could be admitted to a highly selective college today on the basis of his secondary school records, those who defend the present admission practices reply that such cases are the rare exceptions. But the list of individuals who have contributed greatly to society despite mediocre secondary school records is much too long to be ignored. They are not the rare exceptions but rather common exceptions, and they include a number of individuals who have won the Nobel Prize for literature and other awards for conspicuous adult achievement. In any case, a college that refuses to seek out the exceptional individuals who will emerge as leaders, and to provide opportunity for their education, is not accepting its full responsibility. It cannot be called a great institution.

Some highly selective colleges do look for the exceptional individuals, particularly those who have given evidence of creativity, artistic, musical or literary talent, leadership, or athletic ability. But more often they require such evidence *in addition* to good grades and high test scores. The student who has great ability but is introverted and not "well-rounded" is likely to be overlooked.

Most of the highly selective colleges are independent of church or state control. In a day of burgeoning enrollments any independent college with even a modest degree of visibility can easily raise entrance standards if it chooses to do so. It can if it wishes, and if it prefers to keep the enrollment small, deny admission to students scoring lower than 600 or 700 on College Boards or who failed to make A grades in high school. A state college that takes the same step is likely to lose its support from the taxpayers, most of whom were not A students. A church-related school that becomes so highly selective that it refuses to admit reasonably well-qualified members of the church is likely to encounter strong pressures to modify its practices. It seems safe, therefore, to predict that state- and church-related colleges will continue to be less stringently selective than the independent ones. Whether the most selective colleges are also the best colleges in the sense of offering the highest quality of education is at best debatable. It is undoubtedly true that students work harder in a college with high entrance standards because the competition is greater. It is also true that bright students learn a great deal from other bright students. In a selective college the professors are able to make longer and more difficult assignments with confidence that the students will complete them. And, because many people do associate selectivity with quality, the highly selective colleges are better able to attract grants from private donors, the federal government, and foundations. I can testify from my own experience as a staff member of the Ford Foundation that there is a reluctance to make grants to institutions that are less selective and therefore lacking in prestige.

It cannot be assumed that the most selective colleges get the best teachers, for a professor need not be a great teacher or even a good teacher to survive in a college in which all the students are both academically talented and highly motivated. Even if he does no more than make assignments and grade papers, his students will learn. His job is far easier than that of a teacher in a less selective college who must accept responsibility for motivating his students, raising their levels of aspiration, and making difficult ideas clear to them. Selective colleges are likely to attract the kind of teachers who prefer to work exclusively with academically talented students who are easy to teach. Whether these are the best teachers is debatable. And whether students in the selective colleges really learn more than the same students would have learned in less selective colleges is, at best, unproved.

Educational Quality

Though the assessment of institutional quality is a popular pastime, quality—as a trait distinct from either prestige or exclusiveness—proves to be an elusive attribute. Prestige can at least be estimated by counting the number of students who want to get in, selectivity by counting the number the college chooses to keep out. But quality is not so easily measured. The usual approach is to count the number of doctoral degrees held by the faculty and the number of books in the library, to assess the value of the physical plant, and to examine the test scores of the entering freshmen. But all these items are related to input—not output.

The output of a college is its graduates. But we do not know how to measure the qualities of graduates—we are not sure even what these qualities ought to be. And even if they could be identified and measured it would be difficult to prove that they are the result of a student's attendance at a particular college. Mr. X went to Yale; Mr. X became a great man who contributed to the welfare of mankind in a notable way. But we cannot be certain that Mr. X became a great man *because* he went to Yale. It is entirely possible that he might have made the same contribution to mankind had he gone to an obscure university or if, like Lincoln, he never had gone to any college.

If asked to name the best university in the United States a few football buffs who read only the sports pages might say Notre Dame, but many people would say Harvard. If asked to justify the choice they might say: "Because it is big, it has a long and reputable history, lots of money, a big library, and an able faculty, and because several of its alumni have become presidents of the United States."

Asked the name of the best small undergraduate college, the respondents would offer a much wider variety of answers but some knowledgeable people might say "Swarthmore." Asked why they chose Swarthmore, they might say: "Because it is small, has a good faculty, and admits only bright students and because its graduates do well in graduate school." If asked how they know that Swarthmore has a good faculty they would find the question difficult to answer.

It is doubtful that any of these respondents have identified the qualities that make for greatness. There is no convincing evidence that institutional size is related, either positively or negatively, to educational quality. NYU is much larger than Harvard but no one calls it greater. Johns Hopkins and Clark were top-ranking schools when they had only a few hundred students each, but the University of California, which enrolls nearly 100,000 students, also has a good reputation as a graduate institution.

Some of the most prestigious undergraduate colleges are small, but it is at least debatable whether Bennington (with 360 students) or Sarah Lawrence (with 500) offers a better education than Smith with 2300, or that Haverford with 500 men offers a better education than Harvard College, which enrolls 4800 undergraduates.

High salaries, if maintained over a period of time, undoubtedly attract some of the better professors, other things being equal. But other things never are equal and professors, in selecting a position, give consideration to many other attractions, including location, prestige, teaching load, and opportunities for research. Parsons College pays higher salaries than Yale, Princeton, or Stanford but Parsons does not yet appear on anyone's list of quality institutions.

A large endowment provides institutional stability, but some of the most imaginative experimental colleges in the country made their way with almost no endowed funds. Only after their reputations were made did the money begin to roll in, and by that time some of them had become conventional.

A multimillion-volume library is essential for research scholars and useful to graduate students, but for undergraduates a few thousand carefully selected volumes, if easily available, may make for better education. Even if he reads two complete volumes per day throughout his undergraduate years, a student will read no more than 2500 books. Selection is far more important than the numbers listed in the library catalogue. And if books are as hard to find as they are in many research libraries, the student will spend more time locating books than reading them. Thomas Jefferson had only a few hundred books in his library, but because they included some of the greatest books ever written, and because he read them, he was able to write some of the documents upon which our nation rests.

A long line of distinguished graduates dating back over the centuries looks impressive but gives proof only that the institution has been in existence for a long time. Antiquity gives little evidence of present-day educational quality; some of the colleges founded in colonial days are now generally considered second-rate institutions. Some of those founded between 1800 and 1850 are fourth- or fifth-rate, while some of those founded within the last two or three decades command the respect of scholars.

A study of one kind of academic output was made in 1953 by two psychology professors at Wesleyan University under a grant from the Fund for the Advancement of Education. They traced the undergraduate origins of a group of young scholars which had won some postbaccalaureate distinction of a scholarly nature. In their report, *The Younger American Scholar: His Collegiate Origins,* the authors make clear the limitations of the study. "It was decided that the best public indications of future scholarly or scientific promise were the winning of some fellowship, scholarship, or prize on a graduate level in open competition, or the attainment of a Ph.D. or its equivalent." [13] The investigators did not include postdoctorate distinctions, and "no attempt was made to include in our roster individuals who had won distinctions in the fields of medicine, law, or theology if these distinctions were solely confined to these professions and not earned in competition with the general body of graduate students." Achievement in business or government was also excluded.

Most of the institutions that rated highest on the list were small, private liberal arts colleges such as Swarthmore, Oberlin, Haverford, Reed, and Carleton, although Chicago and the California Institute of Technology also rated high. Harvard and Yale fell below these colleges and the state universities still lower— Wisconsin, in thirty-sixth place, led the Big Ten. The University of California was not among the first fifty in over-all ratings.

The higher-ranking colleges made the most of these findings. The resulting publicity led many people to conclude that Swarthmore and Reed were the "best" colleges in the nation. This was a gross misinterpretation of the evidence. No doubt these are excellent colleges, but all that this study proved was that the kind of students that attend them, and survive to graduation, are the kind who do well in graduate schools. Probably they do well for a variety of reasons: they are highly motivated, they had good undergraduate instruction in a college whose undergraduate courses resemble graduate ones, and they were academically talented to begin with. But they were bright even before they entered college—the college cannot take credit for that. A college education enables a student to become better informed and possibly wiser, but it does not substantially alter his IQ. A college that admits only very bright freshmen will have only very bright graduates whether it teaches them much or not. Even if the results are taken at face value, all this study indicates is that *if* the purpose of a college is to be a prep school for graduate schools these are good colleges. It says nothing at all about the success of colleges in preparing students for other kinds of life or for more adult levels of achievement.

Institutional quality has little meaning except when judged in terms of a student's individual talents and his personal goals. The college that is the best choice for one student may be a very bad choice for another. But for the student who knows what he wants, some estimates of quality are possible.

If a student wants a broadly liberal education he is more likely to get it in a college that emphasizes and takes pride in such education than in a university that looks upon liberal education as a sideline. If he wants to become a Wall Street broker, Yale is a better bet than Kansas State, but if he wants to specialize in agriculture, home economics, engineering, or veterinary medicine, Kansas State is a better choice. If he wants to become a public-school teacher he is more likely to find what he needs at Peabody or in any of a number of state colleges than at Princeton. If he would like to have ample time for leisurely reading and quiet contemplation, no matter how brilliant he is, he should avoid the highly selective colleges, most of which are academic pressure cookers. If he wants to be an All-American halfback he should avoid Chicago and will have a better chance in a Big Ten university than in the Ivy League. If he wants to be "where the action is" he will like Berkeley. If he wants a great deal of freedom in his personal life and would resent being required to attend chapel, he should avoid most of the small denominational colleges.

If he wants to enter politics he should be told that in the 90th Congress, which convened in January 1967, all but four of the hundred senators and all but twenty-two of the representatives had some education beyond high school but that they attended all kinds of colleges. Of the senators, 61 per cent received part or all of their higher education in publicly supported institutions. Of the fifty governors in office in 1967, exactly half had attended publicly supported colleges or universities, while both the President and the Vice-President were graduates of such institutions. But geography makes a difference: both senators from Massachusetts are Harvard men, while both of those from the state of Washington are graduates of the University of Washington. It appears that for political aspirants living along the East Coast attendance at a private college gives a slight advantage but that for those who plan to run for office in the West or Middle West attendance at a state university provides a background more attractive to voters. It seems doubtful that any one of the Kennedys would have been elected to office by the voters of Massachusetts if he had attended a western state college or that Lyndon Johnson would have been elected by the voters of Texas if he had returned from college with a Harvard accent.

For those who wish to become writers, the choice of a college does not seem to matter. Sinclair Lewis went to Yale, Robert Frost went to Harvard, where he lasted less than a year; Carl Sandburg went to Lombard College, William Faulkner briefly attended the University of Mississippi, Ole Rölvaag studied and taught at St. Olaf College, Mark Van Doren went to the University of Illinois, Willa Cather graduated from the University of Nebraska, but Hemingway did not go to college.

It is entirely possible for a student to get a good education in any college, or for that matter without going to college. Even the poorest college has more books than he will have time to read. It is the very rare college that does not have at least a few very able teachers on its faculty. If he chooses his professors with care (as he still can do in a college that is too poor to purchase computers to assign him to his classes) he can make the most of such talent as exists. If most of his classmates do not possess great academic talent, his own ability will stand out all the more, and as a result he will get more attention from the faculty. And his opportunities to develop his own leadership potential will be greater in a college in which he does not have to compete with classmates who were all presidents of the high school student body.

This is not to say that the choice of a college does not matter. For some students it probably matters a great deal. But we know all too little about just how it matters and what difference the choice does make. The student who is poorly motivated, or who lacks intellectual curiosity, will not survive in a rigorous college and will not learn very much in a weak college. But the well-motivated student who wants to know and to understand will educate himself no matter what college he attends. All a good college can do is make it easier for him.

The student who is denied admission to "the college of his choice" rarely thanks the admission board that turned him down, but he should, for the probability is high that his choice was unwise. The student who is not really qualified for admission to a highly selective college, but is admitted because he has influential parents who are able to bring pressure, is likely to have a hard time when he faces the rigorous competition. The properly qualified student, who survives until graduation in a highly selective college, will probably be prepared to do well in graduate school; but whether he will be better educated or more wise ten years after graduation than he would have been had he attended a less selective institution remains unproved.

Students who find it necessary to attend colleges that are neither highly selective nor prestigious—as the great majority must —need not fear that they will be seriously or permanently handicapped. A few years after they graduate no one will ask where they went to college and few will care. When they apply for more responsible jobs that require maturity the principal question will be, "What have you done since graduation?"

Quality in Graduate Education

It is somewhat easier to assess the quality of graduate schools than that of undergraduate liberal arts colleges because the goals of graduate education are more sharply defined and the number of institutions is much smaller. The most recent comprehensive study of the subject is that sponsored by the American Council on Education, the results of which were published in a volume edited by Allan M. Cartter, published in 1966, titled *An Assessment of Quality in Graduate Education.*[14]

This volume does not claim to be more than a survey and analysis of the opinion of 900 department chairmen, 1700 outstanding senior scholars and scientists, and 1400 younger academicians concerning the relative quality of the education provided in American graduate schools. The study covered thirty academic fields but did not include medicine, law, or other professional fields except engineering.

The respondents were asked two questions:

A. Which of the terms below best describes your judgment of the *quality of the graduate faculty* in your field at each of the institutions listed? Consider only the scholarly competence and achievements of the present faculty: 1. distinguished, 2. strong, 3. good, 4. adequate, 5. marginal, 6. not sufficient to provide acceptable doctoral training, 7. insufficient information.

B. How would you rate the institutions below if you were selecting a graduate school to work for a doctorate in your field today? Take into account the accessibility of faculty and their scholarly competence, curricula, educational and research facilities, the quality of graduate students and other factors which contribute to *the effectiveness of the doctoral program:* 1. extremely attractive, 2. attractive, 3. acceptable, 4. not attractive, 5. insufficient information.

There followed a list of each of the universities among the 106 in the survey that had awarded one or more doctorates in the particular field of study within the preceding decade.

The results of the questionnaires were reported by Mr. Cartter in statistics and carefully guarded language. But when the report was released to the public, California newspapers proclaimed that the Berkeley campus of the University of California had been found to be "the best university in the country." Harvard, which

had a better claim because it had scored above Berkeley in everything except engineering, which is not taught at Harvard, gave
less attention to the report, probably because Harvard has never
doubted that it is the best of all possible universities. But other
universities, including Yale, Stanford, Columbia, Michigan, and
Wisconsin, received wide publicity for the fact that they had
been found to be in the top five or the top ten. Many readers
were led to believe that these findings provided reliable evidence
of over-all institutional quality. The pecking order among universities was reinforced and the efforts of other institutions to
rise in quality and prestige were made more difficult.

It is regrettable that many naïve college applicants and their
parents accepted this study—on the basis of newspaper accounts
—as indicative of undergraduate educational equality, even
though the ACE made no such claim. Perhaps there is a positive
correlation between the quality of a graduate school and the quality of the undergraduate college in the same university—no one
really knows. But it is entirely possible that the correlation is
negative because the easiest way for a university to build up its
graduate school is to divert its funds and other resources from the
undergraduate to the graduate schools. This diversion of funds is
particularly apparent in the upward-striving institutions that are
eager to develop doctoral programs but lack the necessary resources. It is less apparent in the older universities that had prestigious colleges before their graduate schools came into existence.

It is probably true that the presence of a good graduate school
on a university campus provides intellectual stimulation for both
students and professors. This is especially true in the sciences in
which new knowledge is accumulating rapidly, less true in the
humanities where change is slower and the stability of knowledge
greater. It is true also that some graduate-school professors give
stimulating lectures to undergraduates, though their number is
smaller than one might wish. But in a university that stresses
graduate programs and research, the undergraduate is likely to
get less than his share of attention unless the liberal arts college
has a faculty as well as an administration of its own.

For those selecting a graduate school, the Cartter report gives fairly reliable evidence of quality as it is perceived by scholars qualified to judge it. According to this evidence, the nation's best graduate schools are found in a small number of universities most of which are located along the East and West coasts and in the Great Lakes region. Some distinguished departments, however, are found in a much larger number of universities located in almost all parts of the nation. It is hardly surprising that the best graduate programs are found in the universities with the most ample financial support and the highest salaries to professors.

PART TWO
STUDENTS OF A NEW ERA

7.   Six Million Students

Why They Go to College

As we enter the last third of the twentieth century, some six million young Americans are enrolled, on a part or full-time basis, in the nation's institutions of higher learning—a higher number, and a larger proportion of the population, than has been so engaged in any other nation at any other time in history. The number is expected to rise to eight or nine million by 1980, after which it may decline slightly for a time because of the sharply falling birthrate of the sixties.

Since no one is required to go to college—compulsory school laws do not apply at the higher levels—these high figures reflect the individual decisions of young men and women that higher education is something they want and need. They come to college for a variety of reasons, some of which are sharply at odds with the goals proposed by educational philosophers. Few freshmen are deeply concerned about assuring the continuity of our culture; their goals are personal. Though some hope to expand their intellectual horizons by learning more about the nature of the world and of man, many enter college because their friends are going, because it is a part of the family tradition, or because it seems the only thing to do after graduating from high school. Many are eager to participate in the social life that is a part of the college experience. Primarily, however, the growing demand for higher education reflects the desire of individuals for a higher standard of living and for ever greater status, prestige, and security. The American people want a better life and believe that education provides the open door.

Whatever their motives may be, most students are in pursuit of a status symbol called a degree—a piece of synthetic parchment stating that the holder is now a "bachelor," "master," or "doctor," and entitled to "all the rights and privileges appertaining thereunto." Both the students and their parents are convinced that the possession of such a document is essential if one is to achieve his goals in life. This belief, which has been encouraged by vast amounts of publicity, is rapidly becoming a part of the conventional wisdom. And to many the symbol has come to seem more important than the education it is presumed to represent.

To obtain his degree, each student will stand for many hours in registration lines and then sit through 1200 to 1800 fifty-minute lectures. Whether the lectures are brilliant, scholarly, pedantic, or dull—and he will hear all kinds—he will respond by filling many notebooks with notes, most of which he will never be able to decipher. If his college offers small classes he will take part in many class discussions, some on a high intellectual level and others that will be little more than a sharing of ignorance. He will write thirty or forty term papers, complete with footnotes and all the other apparatus of scholarship, which will be read by no one except the instructor and not always by him. He will labor through hundreds of quizzes, tests, and examinations, most of which will be scored by a computer. He will read perhaps forty textbooks and hundreds of other books; some of these he will wisely forget and a few he will remember all his life. But a year after graduation it is unlikely that he will recall even the names of the authors of 10 per cent of his textbooks, most of which he will have sold as soon as the course was completed. He will often wonder if it is all worthwhile, and there is about an even chance that he will decide to drop out before he gets his first degree.

Even though a substantial part of the cost of his education will be paid by the college from endowments, or by the state through taxation, the student or his parents will make financial sacrifices to keep him in college. Board, room, travel, clothing, books, fees, and incidentals will cost anywhere from $4000 to $15,000 or more for his four undergraduate years. Moreover, the student will sacrifice most of the $12,000 to $20,000 he might have earned had he been employed on a full-time basis during those years.

The willingness of students and their families to make these sacrifices is evidence of high motivation that reflects strong social pressures. But what a student hopes to gain from a college education—or from the degree that symbolizes it—depends on his family background. If he is one of the first in his family to enter college he probably believes that a college degree will help him "get ahead in the world"—to rise in social position and enjoy a higher standard of living than his ancestors. But he also knows that if he fails to graduate his parents are not likely to look upon his failure as a tragedy. They know that, if necessary, he can get a job without a college education just as many of his friends have done.

The student whose parents are college graduates (particularly one whose father is a successful professional man or business executive) has a different motivation. He cannot reasonably hope that a degree, or even two or three degrees, will enable him to rise in social position or to achieve a higher income than that of his father. He must graduate from college with a good record just to maintain the family's place in the world. To him and his family it is not enough just to go to college; he must go to the "right" college. Failure to be admitted to that college causes embarrassment to him and his family; failure to graduate seems a tragedy. Consequently he is under greater pressure to continue even though he has relatively less to gain from college than does the student from a family without a college tradition.

As more people go to college the value of a degree will depreciate just as the value of a high school diploma has decreased in recent decades, because no symbol possessed by millions can give assurance of high status. In 1900, when only 10 per cent of the young people went through secondary school, a high school diploma provided entrée into the white-collar class; today, with some 75 per cent completing high school, many high school graduates enter skilled and semi-skilled trades. In the past a college degree has provided the open door to the upper-middle class that is composed largely of professional people and executives. But when the time comes that from one-half to two-thirds of all adults are college graduates (as compared to today's 10 per cent) the degree will mean less socially because many people with such degrees will be engaged in subprofessional and nonexecutive positions. Still it is not likely that many of those who go to college and stay to receive their degrees will ever regret it. For twentieth-century Americans who want to participate fully in the opportunities of the contemporary world, college is increasingly a part of the essential background.

Who Needs a College Degree?

In the past, neither a college degree nor the formal education it is intended to represent has been essential for those who wished to make notable contributions to mankind, earn a high income, or achieve distinction at the highest levels. Two-thirds of the Presidents of the United States have been college graduates; they have come from such obscure colleges as Ohio Central, Dickinson, Union, and Southwest Texas State Teachers, and from better-known small colleges such as William and Mary, Kenyon, Bowdoin, and Amherst, as well as from Harvard, Yale, and Princeton. But some of the most distinguished Presidents, including Washington, Jackson, and Lincoln had much less formal education. Thomas Edison had no higher education, nor did such industrialists as Carnegie, Rockefeller, or Ford. Until recently it has been possible for many men to achieve distinction in business, industry, government, and the arts with only an elementary education.

This is the story of the past. Young men and women now in school, most of whom will live at least a third of their lives in the twenty-first century, face a different prospect. The doors of opportunity are increasingly closed to those lacking diplomas and degrees. In some cases the barriers are arbitrary, but for the ambitious young man or woman they are all too real.

This does not mean, as some students believe, that "you can't get a decent job without a college education." The great majority of "decent jobs" require no higher education, even in this automated age. Truck drivers, electricians, carpenters, locomotive engineers, mechanics, and men in many of the other skilled trades hold responsible jobs and make good incomes without college degrees.

But it is true that a large and growing number of vocations are now completely closed to those without a college education. This is obviously true of law, medicine, teaching, social work, engineering, architecture, and, in most churches, the ministry. As other professional and subprofessional groups raise their standards and strengthen their positions, more vocations will be added to the list. Many civil service jobs require a college education, and it is becoming increasingly difficult to get a commission in the armed forces without a degree. It is not true, and is not likely ever to be true, that a college education is required for success in business, but it is true that the young man who wants to start out as a junior executive in a major corporation is severely handicapped without a degree and finds it easier to get his first job if he has made a good record in a college the corporation considers prestigious.

It is unlikely that there will ever be formal educational requirements for elective office in a democratic nation, but as the total number of educated voters increases, the chances of an individual who runs for high political office without a higher education will be reduced. Even today, only 26 of the 535 senators and representatives in the 90th Congress had no education beyond high school and most of these are older men. It seems a safe prediction that Harry Truman will go down in history as the last man to have reached the White House without a college degree and that congressmen without college education will become increasingly rare.

Higher education is not a prerequisite for success in such highly paid vocations as show business and professional athletics. In the past it has almost seemed to be a handicap, but that is changing. College graduates are no longer considered curiosities in Hollywood and even the chorus line of a Broadway musical is now likely to include one or two high-kicking girls from Sarah Lawrence or Bennington, or possibly even Vassar. The kind of illiterates made famous by Ring Lardner are becoming rarer in baseball since Jackie Robinson demonstrated that neither a Phi Beta Kappa key nor a dark skin is an absolute barrier to success. The majority of Olympic track and field stars are college men. Professional football teams are staffed almost entirely with college graduates because the professional leagues have found it profitable to let the colleges provide their farm teams. But the athletic boy who never made it through the eighth grade still finds the door to success wide open in wrestling and boxing.

Most young men and women now entering journalism are college graduates, but I do not know of any publisher who makes a degree a fixed requirement for writing or editing. Neither the editor nor the reader cares whether the author of a novel or a book of poems has been to college. The composer of a symphony or the painter of a canvas is not asked to present academic credentials; he is judged by his work. It seems unlikely that the arts, music, or literature will ever be closed to those lacking formal education, and it would be tragic indeed if decisions about the merits of artistic production should ever be influenced by the education of the artist. Still, it seems certain that the proportion of artists and writers holding degrees will steadily increase because more and more of the talented individuals will go to college.

The kind of higher education that provides the best preparation for employment depends, obviously, on the vocation selected. What is not always so obvious is that the kind that best prepares a young graduate for his first job often is poor preparation for the more responsible jobs that may become available to him when he is more mature and has gained greater experience.

The employment officer who interviews a candidate for his first job is likely to ask "What can you do?" and the job is more likely to be offered if the answer is clearly related to some kind of formal training. At this point in a career, a liberal education is less helpful than a technical education that provides specific know-how. But a decade or two later, when the individual becomes eligible for a more broadly responsible job, narrowly specialized education is not enough. An editor, a foundation official, a senator, or a top executive in business needs the ingredients of a truly liberal education. It is not enough for him to be competent in a specialty—he must be able to see problems in broad perspective as a step toward making sound judgments.

A great deal of nonsense has been disseminated by people who ought to know better about the value in dollars of a college degree. Students have been told that because of their college education their lifetime incomes will be increased by $150,000 to $250,000 or more. These figures are arrived at by comparing the average earnings of those who go to college with those who do not, without regard to possible differences in intelligence, special aptitudes, motivation, or opportunities afforded by the individual's family. It is true, or has been true in the past, that the average income of college graduates is substantially higher than the national average for all workers and that the mean for the alumni of Harvard, Yale, and Princeton is higher than that of graduates of obscure institutions. But such conclusions must be drawn with care.

It is entirely possible that the alumni of the Big Three have high incomes because these colleges attract and admit more than their share of the kind of boys who would achieve high incomes no matter where they got their education. The Rockefellers of the third and fourth generations after John D. are graduates of prestigious colleges and all have very high incomes that help raise the averages for their respective graduating classes. But it does not follow that their alma maters can legitimately take credit for their financial success or that a boy from a Kansas farm who goes to the same college can expect to do as well. To be sure, there are only a few Rockefellers, but there are many other wealthy families whose sons will take over the family business. And it takes only a few multimillion-dollar incomes to raise the averages considerably and to give a distorted view of what a college can promise.

The incomes of graduates of state colleges and universities provide a fairer indication of what a student can expect to gain financially from a college degree because most of the graduates of such institutions are dependent upon their own earning capacities for their incomes. Though the figures available are confused and confusing, it seems a fair guess that the graduate of a state college can reasonably expect, by the time he is forty, to have an income about 50 per cent higher than that of the average individual without a college education. But this is not to say that it will be that much more than the *same individual* would have made without a college education. On that subject we have very little evidence.

We do know that some of the professions that employ large numbers of college graduates, such as teaching, the ministry, social work, and nursing, offer incomes no higher than those in some of the skilled trades that do not require a college education. The boy who goes to college and then enters one of these professions may discover that his income is no higher than that of his father, who is a truck driver, plumber, machinist, or locomotive engineer. A college education gives assurance of a higher income only for those who choose the scarcer vocations, who become business executives, or who enter the fee-taking professions such as medicine. But at best, the desire to make money is a poor reason for going to college.

The question "Who needs a college education?" is different, of course, from "Who needs a college degree?" Those who are willing to think about the education itself instead of the symbol can find many reasons for urging everyone with the necessary intellectual capacity to go to college, whether or not he plans to seek a job that requires a degree. It may be hard to prove that higher education makes better mothers, wiser voters, or more enlightened citizens, but it seems reasonable to assume that it does—if it does not, it is doubtful that the education was truly liberal. It is equally difficult to prove that a college background enables one to live a fuller, richer life, but there is sufficient positive evidence to justify the decision that anyone of high intelligence who fails to go to college will miss a great deal and will find it difficult to gain equivalent experience elsewhere. For most Americans the evidence seems persuasive enough. There is little doubt that in the future a large proportion of young Americans will seek some form of higher education whether or not it is essential to their vocational goals.

The Class of 1970

In the fall of 1966, the American Council on Education made a study of more than 200,000 freshmen in 251 colleges, universities, and technological institutions. Each student completed an elaborate questionnaire covering a wide range of biographical data and personal opinion. The answers were statistically weighted to produce norms for the entire freshman population of more than a million students. The results provide a profile of the group that hopes to graduate in the class of 1970.

Nearly half the group (47 per cent) estimated their family incomes at more than $10,000 a year, and only 20 per cent placed the figure below $6000. Forty-six per cent said their fathers had some college education and 27 per cent reported that their fathers were college graduates; the comparable figures for their mothers were 38 per cent and 18 per cent. But most of the students expected to complete more years of schooling than their parents. Eighty-nine per cent expected to receive their bachelor's degrees, 40 per cent planned to go on for their master's degrees, and 10 per cent planned to go on for the academic doctorate.

The findings confirm the growing impression that today's college students are turning their backs on business as a career. Only 12 per cent of the freshmen planned to go into business, while 22 per cent planned to become elementary or high school teachers, 5 per cent looked forward to medical careers, 4 per cent to law, and 9 per cent planned to become engineers. But fewer than 2 per cent planned to become college professors and only 1 per cent wanted to be clergymen. Seven per cent hoped to become artists or performers, while the vocational goals of the others were scattered among a large number of vocations. But 21 per cent hoped to spend some time in the Peace Corps or VISTA before settling down to permanent jobs.

There can be little doubt that many of these students face disappointment. Insofar as we can predict from the recent past, not more than 40 per cent of them will graduate with their classmates in the spring of 1970 and no more than 60 per cent will ever receive a bachelor's degree from any college. The others will drop out for any of several reasons, including an inability to do college work of an acceptable quality.

If 10 per cent of entering freshmen should complete the Ph.D. the number of such degrees granted annually in the seventies would be well over 100,000. Even the most optimistic predictions do not provide for more than 30,000 to 40,000 such degrees per year, and even that would double the number granted in the late sixties. And many who do not wish to become businessmen will undoubtedly enter upon business careers.

Those who wish to become elementary or secondary teachers have a good chance of attaining their goals because the teaching profession will probably need at least 20 per cent of the college graduates of the seventies. In the past the proportion has been much higher than this, but the demand for teachers is not growing nearly so rapidly as the number of college graduates. But to staff our colleges we shall need substantially more than the 2 per cent who now anticipate college teaching as a career. To fill the gap, some of those who now plan to become research scientists and engineers, and many of those who wish to be artists, will instead become teachers.

Responses to questions about their plans for financing their college education make it clear that these students come from an affluent society. Only 8.6 per cent said that financing their education was a major concern to them, and only 8.3 per cent said that employment during the school year was their chief source of income, though 28.3 per cent said they relied heavily on summer employment. Scholarships were reported to be the major support for 14.6 per cent, but 58.3 per cent said that their major support came from their parents. It appears that "working your way through college" is less common today than it was a generation or two ago.

Questions about their activities during the past year brought forth some interesting responses. A surprising 63.5 per cent said they had attended church frequently, 38.5 per cent that they said grace before meals frequently, and 48.6 per cent had prayed often. Fifty-three and a half per cent had drunk beer, while only 16.6 per cent smoked cigarettes frequently; 20.6 per cent had cribbed on examinations; 37.7 per cent had gambled with cards or dice. (The report does not say how many of the same students engaged in these various activities.)

When asked about their objectives in life, 43.8 per cent expressed a hope to become well off financially, but 66 per cent said they hoped to become "an authority in my field" and 68.5 per cent expressed a desire "to help others who are in difficulty." Only 13.5 per cent wished to become outstanding athletes and 10.8 per cent hoped to achieve in a performing art.

Though questionnaires of this kind reveal something less than the ultimate truth, these responses give no reason for despair about the younger generation. The class of 1970 seems to be made up of fairly normal people who are apparently somewhat more socially conscious and less governed by economic motives than their parents. But a deeper probe might reveal more significant differences.

8. A New and Different Generation

Three Views

When old-timers undertake to assess the faults and virtues of the young they are likely to take one of three basic positions. The most venerable is that the younger generation is going to the dogs, a view that was popular with the Greeks and Romans and has appeared in the literature of nearly every period since classical times. Pundits throughout the ages have proclaimed that the youth of their day were lazy, immoral, irresponsible, and dishonest. They have predicted that these young people would never be able to accept adult responsibilities and that consequently civilization would decline. And they have not always been mistaken. Greek culture did fall into ruin; the Roman Empire, after a period of moral dissolution, declined and fell apart.

It is possible that the twilight of Western civilization is upon us, as Spengler predicted, but a half century after his *Decline of the West* appeared his predictions still seem premature. There is indeed much disorder and conflict within our culture as well as a notable loss of confidence in the future, but there is also still a great deal of rugged vitality. Though in some members of the younger generation, as well as in some of our own generation, there is evidence of a loss of nerve and of the kinds of moral degeneration that accompanied the fall of Rome, there is as yet no clear evidence of a collapse in the culture as a whole. If the culture eventually does disintegrate, there will be no logical reason for blaming the younger generation, or the older generation, for the collapse. The causes will go deeper and farther back.

A second view, frequently expressed by optimistic commencement speakers, is that his is the best of all possible generations— that today's students are more virtuous, better motivated, and more enlightened than any that have gone before; and that as a result we can face the future with confidence that a better world lies just ahead. This view is too blandly optimistic for my taste; it ignores too many symptoms of profound illness within the society, including some segments of the younger group. There is no very good reason to believe that this younger generation, when it moves into positions of responsibility, will be able to solve the world's problems much better than we have done.

A third view, popular with elderly professors of the Mr. Chips variety, is that one generation is very much like another. Young people must always go through a period of adolescent rebellion during which they find it difficult to accept the rules and regulations that govern adult society; each generation thinks itself the first to have discovered sex and liquor, but this is all just a matter of growing up. According to this view the present generation, a few years after graduation, will become very much like its parents—moderately virtuous, moderately industrious, moderately law-abiding, and moderately stuffy. All it will take is a little time, a job, a marriage certificate, three or four children, and a house bought on the installment plan.

There is, of course, an element of truth in this. Many adolescent rebels do become conservative adults, not because of age but as a result of new responsibilities and a growing vested interest in the *status quo* that makes rebellion seem less desirable. But this view fails to take into consideration the fact that each generation is a product of its own times and develops its special character in response to the pressures, challenges, and opportunities it faces. If today's youth are substantially different from those of earlier days, as I think they are, it is because they have grown to maturity in a different world.

Anxiety in the Midst of Affluence

Today's college students, like human beings everywhere, seek identity for themselves and meaning and purpose for their lives. Like the students of other generations they are eager for success—as they define success—and are concerned about jobs and careers. Like all young people they are in search of temporary or permanent mates. Most of them are thoughtful, serious, and responsible. Some are wise beyond their years.

But such generalizations, even if true as I believe they are, cannot do justice to the infinite variety of individuals among the six million students who inhabit our campuses—they leave significant minorities undescribed and unexplained. Those of us who meet students daily in our classes get an impression of much greater diversity than is apparent to those who read only the headlines about student demonstrations. We know that there is a radical right as well as a radical left. We know that between the two wings stands a much larger group of students who reject both extremes, not because they are unconcerned or unaware, but because they are willing to wait to get an education before setting out to reform the world.

There are, to be sure, still a few students who think it of overwhelming importance to win the big game on Saturday afternoon and some, though a declining number, who are preoccupied with fraternity life. Some still come to college for fun and games. But most of today's students work much harder than their parents did when they were in college—in most colleges they must do so to survive.

While this generation includes all the traits of previous ones, it would be a mistake to assume that today's students do not differ from those of an earlier day. The differences are ones of degree —a significant statistical shift of the central tendency away from some traits and toward others. Some of these differences, as they are perceived by deans of students in a wide variety of colleges and universities, were recently summarized in *The Journal of the Association of Deans and Administrators of Student Affairs*. The editors, after quoting from the comments of a number of deans, conclude:

> In these and other statements can be found common elements which describe the contemporary student and compare him with his predecessors as:
>
> 1. More sophisticated, urbane, cosmopolitan, informal, experienced, affluent.
> 2. Brighter, more knowledgeable, better prepared academically, better scholastically.
> 3. More serious and conscientious in response to greater academic pressure and competition.
> 4. More dissatisfied with the world around him and more aggressive and demonstrative in his protests, more idealistic.
> 5. More insecure and anxious in response to societal complexities, confusion, and pressures, more introspective.
> 6. Dominated by the pragmatism of getting into graduate school, vocational and materialistic in his thinking.
> 7. Courteous, sensitive, honest, fair, and sincere, but relatively unwilling or unlikely to take responsibility for the behavior of his peers.
> 8. Anxious, even determined, to be accepted, appreciated, respected, noticed, and responded to, to make a difference.
> 9. More sensitive to any sign of lack of confidence in his ability to exercise mature judgment or to any attempt at imposition of advice.
> 10. More dedicated to serving others.
> 11. In search of meaningful relationships with others (including adults) and meaningful personal involvement in a variety of activities, especially in the decisions which affect his life.
> 12. Significantly critical and skeptical of established beliefs, customs, values, and authority.
> 13. More actively, personally, and genuinely concerned and better informed about public and world affairs and social problems and issues.
> 14. More caught up in the spirit of searching, especially for

some kind of commitment, and more demanding of the right
to search.

15. More diverse in interests, concerns, and accomplishments.[15]

The students so described are those who were in college in
1967—a group that differs greatly from the students of the previous decade who were often criticized for their lack of involvement and commitment. Indeed, the students of the sixties have
more in common with those of the twenties and thirties than
with those of the forties and fifties. But the deans are right, I
think, in their judgment that today's students are more sophisticated and knowledgeable, more serious and conscientious, as
well as more dissatisfied with the world around them, and more
aggressive and demonstrative than any preceding generation of
students.

In accounting for these differences it is important to remember
what these students, who were born at midcentury, can and cannot remember. The depression of the thirties, World War II,
even the Korean war are things that they read about in history
books, events that seem almost as remote as the Civil War or the
Irish potato famine. They were only infants when the Supreme
Court declared segregation in the schools unconstitutional. They
were in the primary grades when Sputnik was launched and can
scarcely recall a world not circled by astronauts. When they read
the Kinsey reports they know that Kinsey was describing not
their own generation but an older one that included their parents.

Students now in college have lived all their lives in the shadow
of the great bomb. They rarely talk about it; they seem to give
less conscious attention to the threat than did the students of the
fifties, but it lies always in the background. Other generations
have faced terror—the Black Death, the hordes of Genghis Khan,
or the threat of destruction by artillery and poison gas, but this is
the first generation to face the possibility that the human race
may have no future.

More immediate is the prospect of possible engagement in a

strange kind of undeclared war in a far-off land, the necessity for which is not clear to them and the morality of which is a subject of national and international debate. Young men have never welcomed the prospect of being drafted into the armed forces, subjected to military discipline, and sent out to fight, but it was easier for them to accept its inevitability in World War II when there was a greater degree of national agreement that the cause was just. Today's uncertainty makes it easier for them to feel justified in evading the draft. Many students, both undergraduates and graduates, admit that their main reason for staying in school is that if they leave before they marry they are likely to be drafted. But because patriotism is not really dead, and because many are less than certain of the morality of their decision, the evasion is not without psychological conflict and feelings of guilt that often take the overt form of projecting the blame on the older generation or something vaguely called "the Establishment."

And there are other threats: a rising crime rate, a shocking death toll on the highways, racial conflict, and a growing pollution that threatens to make our water undrinkable and our air unbreathable. Students comment ironically on the prospect that we may soon find ourselves standing knee-deep in filth while launching rockets to the moon. And they are aware that the world population is increasing so rapidly (despite the sharply falling birthrate in the United States) that there soon may be standing room only in many parts of the world and not nearly enough food for everyone.

All these threats are made more immediate by television, for a picture of racial violence, crime, or war, seen only a few hours after the event, is far more anxiety-producing than a written account weeks later. There has always been violence in the world, but this is the first generation that—because it has lived from infancy in front of a television set—is never allowed to forget it. The full effect of television has yet to be assessed—perhaps it can never be fully evaluated—but the message that comes to the younger generation through the tube is that this is a violent and evil world.

While all these threats lie in the background, and stir the emotions daily, this generation has grown up in a world of unparalleled affluence. Most of those who reach college have never lived in homes without electric lights, bathrooms, radios, hi-fi sets, air conditioning, and labor-saving devices that their own grandmothers never dreamed of. Theirs has been a world of orange juice, vitamin pills, and unlimited food supplies—they are of the first generation in history to be bombarded by advertisements that boast of food and drink that contain a *minimal* number of calories.

Though poverty still exists in the United States, few of those who reach college have had any personal experience with it. Most of them have never known hunger, the threat of hunger, or hard physical labor as their ancestors knew it. Unemployment as we knew it in the thirties—the inability of competent, educated people to find work of any kind—is something they have read about but cannot really believe. They are confident that except for the possibility of wars or revolutions they can count on full employment throughout their lives and social security and medicare for their old age. They expect to live all their lives in physical comfort surrounded by too much food, too much liquor, and quite possibly too much LSD. But never having known unemployment, poverty, or physical labor, they do not find the prospect of security attractive. They know that the secure life is not the good life. They have only to observe their own parents to discover that physical comfort, luxuries, and an excess of food and drink do not assure happiness, contentment, or an interesting and exciting life. So they ask "Is this all there is?" and when they find that no one has a very good answer they look for something new—for kicks or for a cause. The kick is likely to be marijuana or LSD—liquor is now considered old-fashioned and middle-class. The cause may be almost anything that seems worth doing, provided it will upset the Establishment. And even the many students who choose not to share in either the kicks or the causes find it easy to be tolerant of those who do because they, too, are products of this age of uncertainty in the midst of affluence.

No one can be certain just how much the outlook of this generation has been influenced by the fact that many of their parents and teachers were steeped in relativistic philosophies and permissive views of child-rearing. But many students report that their parents, though often cautious, critical, and worried, have been reluctant to say a firm *no* to anything or to establish clear guidelines for their conduct. Consequently they have grown up in a world without moral boundaries—a world in which the answer given to those who ask for moral judgments is "It all depends." The only way an adolescent can find out what is permissible and what is forbidden or dangerous is to try everything for himself and then make his own judgment of the consequences. For some exceptionally strong individuals this means an exciting kind of freedom; for a larger number, who are uncertain, insecure, and "hot for certainty" as most adolescents are, it is a source of great anxiety.

The reluctance of older people to express moral judgments with confidence, combined with the fact that many older people are now apt to defend the young in all their conflicts with the Establishment, has encouraged young people to believe that their generation is far superior to the old one. This belief has been reinforced by the fact that they have lived in a world in which the popular culture—television, motion pictures, advertising, and much that appears in print—has been dominated by the whims of teen-agers.

This is the *now* generation, steeped in popularized versions of existential philosophies, indifferent to the past, doubtful about the future, and skeptical of the wisdom of older people. Considering the nature of the world they know, with its combination of affluence, opportunities for hedonistic pleasure, and all its uncertainties and fears, it is not surprising that many young people are anxious and troubled. More remarkable is the fact that a great many of them still remain stable, calm, and responsible.

The Many Facets of Student Unrest

This restless generation has challenged the Establishment on a curiously assorted variety of issues: the war in Vietnam, the draft, civil rights, the voting age, the laws restricting the use of liquor and psychedelic drugs, laws governing pornography, and the right of either college authorities or the local police to govern the behavior of students on and off campus. They have demanded the right to dress as they please, to make speeches on any subject, any time and anywhere, to buy contraceptive devices and birth-control pills in college stores. On at least a few campuses some have demanded the right to carry signs bearing four-letter Anglo-Saxon words which are known to everyone but have disappeared from polite usage. On a number of campuses they have demanded the resignation of presidents or deans, protested the dismissal of popular instructors, published the results of student evaluations of faculty members, and demanded a voice in such major policy decisions as requirements for graduation, college budgets, and the selection of faculty members and administrators. And the students who make such demands are, with increasing frequency, the ones who get elected to student body offices and are chosen as editors of the student press.

Of all these challenges and demands, the most widespread, though not the best publicized, is the demand for freedom from the parietal rules of the college or university. It is doubtful that there is a campus anywhere in the United States on which some students have not recently demanded either changes in the regulations or a complete elimination of rules.

Though it is doubtful that any organization can operate without some rules, it is true, as the students charge, that many of the present rules reflect the assumption that students are immature and that a college must act *in loco parentis*. Parents who send their sons and daughters away to college at the age of seventeen or eighteen have traditionally expected the college to see to it that students were properly fed and housed, got enough sleep, lived moral lives, and had opportunities for wholesome recreation. To satisfy these parental expectations, most colleges, in addition to providing supervised food and housing, have established dormitory hours, particularly for girls, provided chaperones for parties, forbidden the use of alcohol, and in some cases have frowned upon smoking and tried to keep dirty jokes out of the student newspaper. Many denominational colleges have required daily chapel attendance and until recently many frowned upon dancing.

All such rules were frequently broken. College deans, who are much more knowledgeable than most students give them credit for being, have usually been willing to look the other way unless the rule-breaking was too persistent or was of a nature that would bring discredit to the college. But the older generation of students, who looked upon rule-breaking as a game, has been replaced by a moralistic younger group that considers rule-breaking hypocritical and demands that the regulations be changed to conform to actual practice.

In response to their demands, the rules have been gradually modified. Colleges that once required girls to be in their rooms at eight o'clock now consider midnight a suitable hour, while those that were always more lenient now do not lock the doors before two in the morning. Some ask only that the girls check in before breakfast, and a few now leave the decision about hours entirely to the students.

In most colleges, smoking now is permitted in dormitory rooms, at meals, and often in college seminars. Most college stores sell cigarettes even in states where it is illegal for those under twenty-one to smoke. But only a few colleges permit liquor to be served to students at college affairs and most make an effort—usually unsuccessful—to keep it out of the dormitories. Many states have laws prohibiting liquor on college campuses and most deny its legal use to those under twenty-one.

Except in a few church-related colleges, dancing is no longer considered a moral issue. The fact that it once was reflected the views of a number of Protestant churches. When, in the early twenties, it was proposed that square dancing be permitted at Wooster College, one faculty member protested on the grounds that "if we allow them to square dance some may be tempted to lapse into the waltz." By the thirties, however, students in most colleges were dancing "cheek to cheek from head to toe" while faculty chaperones looked on. In the fifties the chaperones began to disappear and now are rarely in evidence. But the dancing styles, while perhaps more visually erotic, no longer involve much bodily contact.

Dormitory regulations become steadily more relaxed. A generation ago it was unheard of for students to have dates in dormitory rooms—in girls' dormitories men were never allowed above the first floor. In the fifties a few colleges began to allow students to entertain visitors of either sex in their rooms at specified times—at first only on Sunday afternoons. Gradually the hours have been extended and the doors have closed. Some students now insist that their rooms are their homes, in which they should have the right to entertain visitors at such times as they may choose.

Many students contend that these relaxations of the rules, far-reaching as they have been, are not enough. They insist that the college has no right to exercise any control whatever over their behavior except when they are in class. They demand an end to *in loco parentis* and, because a growing number of their parents support them in their demand, they are likely to get their way.

Students will discover, however, that when college officials renounce their responsibility for student behavior the jurisdiction falls upon the local police and the courts. Students are not exempt from the law, and American college campuses, unlike university campuses in Mexico, South America, and some parts of Europe, are not out-of-bounds for public law-enforcement officers. In the past, students who violated the laws governing liquor, disorderly conduct, and other misdemeanors were often dealt with more gently by college officials than would have been the case if they had not been students and had been directly confronted by the police and the courts. A student who got drunk and smashed the furniture, when his case was handled by a dean, was likely to be placed on probation or possibly suspended for the remainder of the semester. If the dean now hands the responsibility over to the criminal courts, the same student may get six months in jail for the same offense. On one campus where students protested the right of the college officials to fine them $1 for parking illegally

—and won their case—they discovered that the city government, which then accepted the responsibility for enforcing parking regulations, assessed a fine of $10 for parking in the same space. An end to *in loco parentis* will reduce the responsibilities of the college officials considerably. Whether it will prove to be a boon to the students is questionable.

Student restlessness undoubtedly is increased by the uncertainties of the international situation, the moral dilemmas created by the war in Vietnam, and fear of the draft. Students who feel these uncertainties and face these dilemmas are more apt to lash out against the authorities on issues unrelated to the war. Often they express their hostility toward the older generation by demanding changes in the college as well as in the federal government. But the demand for student power over college affairs raises issues that affect faculty members, administrators, and governing boards as well as students because if students are to have more power within the university these other groups will have less. Consequently a discussion of this issue is best reserved for a later chapter that will deal in broader context with the power structure of academic institutions.

Though student restlessness is widespread it is by no means universal. Indeed, such evidence as we have seems to suggest that it is characteristic of a minority rather than a majority. In a poll taken on the Berkeley campus only a few months after the much-publicized disturbances of the fall of 1964, 90 per cent of the students questioned agreed with the statement "Taking everything into account, Cal is a good place to go to school." Eighty per cent expressed satisfaction with the courses, examinations, and professors. According to a press release of 1966, 86 per cent of the students at the University of Wisconsin indicated that they trusted the administration, while only 6 per cent expressed strong dissatisfaction with the quality of the teaching. Even more surprising, only 16 per cent expressed opposition to the war in Vietnam. But even if it is true that the majority of students are not greatly dissatisfied with the *status quo*, the minority—the restless ones—deserve our further attention.

9. The Conspicuous Minorities

It is always a visible minority that gives a generation its special flavor. The minority that captured the attention of the press and aroused the ire of the older generation in the 1920s was made up of boys who wore coonskin coats and drove Stutz Bearcats, coeds who dressed like John Held's flappers, and collegians of both sexes who danced the Charleston till dawn while getting drunk on bathtub gin. These students of the "flaming youth" era broke far more rules than are broken by today's youth because there were more rules to break. They forced changes in the rules. They are remembered because they overthrew the Puritan morality of an earlier day and paved the way for things to come. And they are the grandparents of some of today's students.

But it *was* a minority. Bearcats were rare even at Princeton and unknown on most campuses—where students, if they had cars at all, drove Model T's. At college proms the foxtrot was far more popular than the Charleston, which, though not really very naughty, is much too fatiguing for an entire evening. And throughout the twenties students drank more malted milk than bootleg liquor, which was too expensive for most undergraduate pocketbooks.

The special flavor of the thirties was provided by students who joined picket lines, signed pledges never to take part in any war however just the cause, and, in some cases, renounced their allegiance to the United States and joined the Communist party. Again it was a minority. Throughout the thirties New Dealers were far more numerous on most campuses than Communists, and most of the students knew the difference even if some of their Republican parents did not.

80

The difference between the visible minorities of the twenties and the thirties is notable because each was responding to life in a special period of history. In the twenties—a time of great prosperity and no very obvious international threats—the demand was for personal freedom. Students wanted to burn their candles at both ends without interference from parents, deans of women, or Mrs. Grundy. In the thirties—a time of depression, the Civil War in Spain, and the rise of Hitler—the demand was for an immediate solution to the social, political, and economic problems that threatened the peace and security of the world. And, because of these differences in the problems that they faced, the students of the thirties were distinctly different from those of the previous decades.

During World War II, college enrollments declined sharply, and then, after 1945, the campus was dominated by veterans returning with the aid of the G.I. Bill. The veterans, being older, more mature, and eager to prepare themselves for peacetime employment, established a new tone on college campuses. There was less of the rah-rah spirit, less interest in joining fraternities, and a greater interest in academic achievement. Because many of the veterans were husbands and fathers, colleges found it necessary for the first time to provide housing for families.

The fifties was a curious decade in which students seemed more conservative than older people. They were described as the "silent generation," a group interested mostly in such conventional things as safe jobs that would provide a split-level home in the suburbs with a television set, two cars in the garage and four or five children in the nursery. Many were said to be concerned with retirement plans and other fringe benefits even when they applied for their first jobs. The reason for such conservatism and conventionality would provide the basis for a good book on social psychology that has yet to be written. In any case, they worked hard (and sometimes cheated on examinations) to achieve their goals.

It was not until the sixties that new conspicuous minorities began to emerge—minorities that combined the traits of those of the twenties with those of the thirties and added some new characteristics all their own. Like the students of the twenties they reflect the hedonism made possible by affluence and, in their effort to make the most of that affluence, demand a greater degree of freedom than has ever been known to any generation. But like the students of the thirties, they are deeply conscious of social injustice. And like the students of the late thirties, they face war and the draft, and in their search for a scapegoat may turn against the United States and those responsible for its leadership.

No one is ever likely to call the students of the sixties a silent generation. The most obvious fact about today's minority is its eagerness for public attention and its ability to attract it. In many respects the individuals within the group differ so greatly that it seems necessary to discuss them as several different minorities: the demonstrators, the alienated, the beatniks, the hippies, and the adherents of the New Left. But the lines between these groups cannot be sharply drawn, for some individuals fall into more than a single category.

The Demonstrators

On a typical October afternoon, while the great majority of the nation's six million college students are busily engaged in educational activities in classrooms, libraries, or laboratories, a small minority is out in the street carrying signs instructing their elders to make love, not war, demanding the reinstatement of a dismissed instructor, denouncing the President of the United States, condemning the dean of students, or demanding an immediate end to some social injustice. And when newsmen report the day's activities in the press or on television this small minority gets most of the attention. Such is the nature of news.

Various estimates have been made of the number of students taking part in demonstrations. At Berkeley about 900 took part in the 1964 sit-in at Sproul Hall—approximately 3.5 per cent of the student body. The number present during other demonstrations on that campus has been estimated as high as 3500, though it is not clear how many of these were participants and how many were onlookers. But such large numbers are rare even at Berkeley and unheard of on other campuses. Many students consider the demonstrations ridiculous and will have no part in them. Most students, however firmly they may believe in causes, have not taken to demonstrating as a way of life.

The demonstrators are able to command attention out of all proportion to their numbers because of their highly sophisticated and newsworthy techniques, which include direct confrontations with administrators and law-enforcement officers as well as such forms of passive resistance as sit-downs and going limp when arrested. Often the press and television stations are notified in advance in order that the demonstrations may have full coverage. The demonstrators are well aware of what makes news.

When Al Capp was asked in a televised interview whether he thought today's younger generation was any worse than his own he replied in the negative. "We were just as ignorant and repulsive as they are," he said, "but nobody listened to us." Today, it seems, everybody is listening. While the calmer and wiser students get no attention whatever, those who demonstrate can be sure that their opinions will be widely quoted in the press and that their pictures will appear on television. It is an ironic fact that the leaders of the Berkeley "Free Speech" movement were allowed greater freedom of speech and given greater opportunity to make their views known to a nationwide and worldwide audience than is usually available to university presidents or U.S. Senators. Their pictures appeared in national picture magazines, their complaints were aired in hundreds of newspapers, and their articles appeared in magazines that reached millions of readers. Freedom of speech is one thing that they were not denied.

It should not be assumed, however, that attention-getting is the primary aim of all the demonstrators or that they are merely giving vent to personal frustrations or maladjustments. Many young people and some older ones take part in demonstrations because they have become aware of social injustice, are not yet in a position to deal effectively with it, and are not willing to wait. "What else can we do?" they ask plaintively. One student leader reflected the views of many when he said: "We demonstrate because we live in a corrupt society which has grown insensitive to human suffering and we can't sit back and allow things to continue that way."

Those with a longer historical perspective are not likely to agree that our world is more corrupt than that of the past or that men today are more insensitive to evil than their ancestors. In long periods of the past slavery was accepted as normal by the young as well as by the old, children were forced to work long hours in factories, sailors were treated with the utmost brutality by their officers, the insane were left to rot away in dungeons—and no one seemed to care or even to be aware. Today we are aware and we do care. The students, being better informed, are more sensitive than those of earlier times, and because they live in a free nation they can express their disapproval whether or not they have a quick and effective solution to offer. But today's students are not the first to find it necessary to live in "a world we never made." All of us, of whatever age, must live in such a world, for no individual can hope to make more than a slight change for the better in our complex society. And whether they like it or not, the student demonstrators are a part of the society that they call corrupt and insensitive.

Though demonstrations rarely deal directly or effectively with the problems of the world, they can, if the causes are wisely chosen, be useful in calling attention to injustices. In any case, the right to protest is a fundamental human right guaranteed by the U.S. Constitution. It must be protected on the campus as well as elsewhere in the nation.

But the right to criticize the demonstrators is also fundamental. Students who make a public show of their protests cannot reasonably expect to be immune from public criticism, nor can they reasonably contend that all those who criticize their actions are reactionary, stupid, or uninformed. Since they want to be treated as adults they must expect to be criticized as adults and not to be given special treatment on the basis of assumed immaturity or lack of experience.

Those who would strike a blow for freedom must take care to identify the true enemies of freedom lest they confuse the issue by lashing out at the wrong targets. Many of the student demonstrators have done just that and have thereby made their demonstrations ineffective.

Those who protest, criticize, or demonstrate must be judged both on the basis of the causes selected and on the basis of the methods employed. Students who demand civil rights for all citizens and equality of treatment for minority groups have a good cause that is shared by many older people. They are on the side of the Constitution, the Supreme Court, the President, the Congress, and the majority of the American people. But though their cause is legitimate, their attacks are often misdirected. They should criticize the minority that blocks our efforts to achieve these goals instead of heaping their scorn on the entire older generation that has done more to advance civil rights and racial equality than any other generation in history.

Those who demand better instruction and more attention to undergraduates also have a good cause. It is true that the status symbols of academia are rigged against good teaching—the highest rewards go to professors who give their time to other things. Every university has some professors who are contemptuous of undergraduates and do not want to teach them. Students are right in calling attention to these facts and demanding a change. I hope they get it. But they are not likely to accomplish this by blasting the administrators; because in most of the better institutions, decisions about promotions are made by faculty committees. Administrators merely give formal approval to decisions already made.

While some of the causes espoused by student demonstrators are sound, others are highly questionable. And some of the methods employed go beyond the constitutional guarantee while others, which may be within the limits of the law, are inappropriate in institutions of higher learning.

Students on a number of campuses, aided and abetted by dropouts and nonstudents, have booed, jeered, and threatened to assault the Secretaries of State and of Defense and other government officials who have been invited to the campus to explain and defend government policy. They have lashed out wildly against college administrators, boards of regents, the nation's military establishment, the police, the courts, the President of the United States, who was hanged in effigy just off one campus, and the Vice-President, who has narrowly escaped mob attacks on several campuses.

Those who engage in such activities are vulnerable on at least three counts: their techniques are those of an insensate mob rather than those of intellectuals who think for themselves and act rationally as individuals; in many cases they are demanding simple solutions to enormously complex problems for which there can be no simple solutions; and by their actions they are denying the right of free speech to those whose views differ from their own. The college administrator who takes official action against students who lead such activities is not denying civil rights—he is protecting the civil rights of the speakers the students will not allow to speak. And the student government that fails to take appropriate action has demonstrated its inability to govern its own members.

Full debate on issues of both local and national policy is a legitimate and essential part of the democratic process. Students should take full part in that debate, bringing to bear all the knowledge that has come to them as a part of their higher education. But they should be aware that debate is an intellectual activity which requires listening to the views of others as well as defending one's own. Booing a speaker, creating such a din that he cannot be heard, or threatening mob attacks against him is not a debate and is not a part of the democratic process. It is a denial both of human rights and of the principles of higher learning. It has no place on a college campus.

The fact that the most virulent criticism of student demonstrations has appeared in the conservative press has led many students to believe that all the demonstrations have the approval of enlightened citizens and that anyone who opposes any demonstration must be politically reactionary. But many enlightened liberals also doubt that the kind of demonstrations that result in hysteria or threats of mob attacks are appropriate in an intellectual community such as a university ought to be. The case against such demonstrations was stated by the distinguished English man of letters, J. B. Priestley.[16] After admitting that he was once a student himself, Priestley says:

> I didn't see then—and have never seen since—why young men in universities, turning themselves into mischievous and sometimes dangerous mobs, should be treated indulgently, as if they were quite different from mobs of garage hands, apprentice fitters, or bus drivers. Indeed, there is a case for more severity. Students are not supposed to be ignorant and stupid. If they are, then they should be sent home and not receive higher education at public expense. . . . They should be the last and not the first to create howling destructive mobs. . . .
>
> It is not the occasional "rags" that get out of hand that I am thinking about right now; it is the so-called "demonstrations" that seem to make an appearance every few nights on the TV news. I do not care whose side they are supposed to be on, I am more and more depressed and revolted by these idiot processions, with their banners and slogans and mindless grinning faces, on their way to break windows, smash cars, burn furniture, and books, terrify women and children, and to reduce international law, custom and sensible usages to chaos. . . . It is all very odd, bewildering, really rather frightening, for while we can just about deal with it today, what will it be like tomorrow? No sooner do we appear to have made the world safer than a strange and half-mad gleam comes into its eyes. The young arrive eager not to create but to destroy. The students never march to build a house but only to knock one down. . . . And though I am familiar with all the usual explanations—H-Bomb, no religion, bad homes, and irresponsible parents, dead-end jobs, boring environment, and the rest—I remain puzzled, never entirely convinced, still wondering if there might not be some unknown factor, a vast X in the dark. Meanwhile, I think I could take some newsreel footage show-

ing me students making something instead of breaking something—or even just studying.

It would obviously be unfair to apply Priestley's judgments to the large number of students who have demonstrated peacefully and within the law, making their opinions known without physically attacking anyone or destroying property. But the number of citizens who share Priestley's views is sufficiently large to pose a serious threat to the necessary continued support for higher education from both public and private sources. There can be little doubt that the public reaction to the California demonstrations played a large part in making possible the election of a conservative governor who has promised to "do something about the mess at Berkeley" and who, after election, took steps to cut the budget for higher education and to cause the dismissal of an able and liberal university president.

There is a growing danger that the protest and demonstrations of the student activists will turn large segments of the public against both students and the institutions of learning and will result in a reluctance to provide the support—both moral and financial—on which higher education depends. Already the impression is widespread that college students are less disciplined, less patriotic, less committed to the democratic process, and less willing to listen to both sides of an argument than other segments of the population. Though this impression results from the activities of only a small minority and is in part a misinterpretation of the evidence, it provides fuel for the anti-intellectualism and antagonism toward the world of scholarship that has always been an underlying fact of American life. Educators cannot safely ignore the threat, because the higher learning in America cannot prosper without public support.

A large part of the blame for the present public misconception of the views held by academic men and their students must be accepted by the silent majority of professors and students who *are* committed to the democratic process, who are willing to listen to both sides without booing or jeering, who accept the

necessity in a free nation for law-enforcement officers, administrators, and a federal government, and who are willing to accept
the responsibilities of citizenship even to the point of entering the
armed forces if necessary—but who have so far remained silent
instead of making their views publicly known. Until the majority
speaks out, the demonstrators will continue to give the impression that they and only they represent the views of those within
the institutions of higher learning.

The Alienated, the Beatniks, and the Hippies

Alienation is a word currently fashionable not only with literary critics but also with psychologists and sociologists who write
about today's youth. Perhaps it should be classified as one of the
"vogue words" identified by Fowler that owe their popularity to
the joy of showing that one has acquired them and to the ease
with which they can be substituted for any one of several more
precise words, thus saving the trouble of choosing the right one.
In any case it seems clear that some of those who write about college students use the word too loosely.

Political protest, however vigorous, is not symptomatic of
alienation—George Washington, who led a revolutionary war,
was not an alienated youth. Some of those who protest government policy today are responsible members of the Establishment.
Nor is the demand for civil rights and racial equality an evidence
of alienation. Those who make such demands are on the side of
the majority of the American people. Those who reject the
larger society but join a subculture such as that of the beatniks,
conform to the customs of that subculture, and find friends within it are not really alienated. The alienated individual rejects the
human race, wants no part of society, and conforms to nothing.

For more than a century the word *alienation* has meant serious
mental illness; in psychiatry and in law an alienist is a physician
who specializes in the diagnosis of individuals classifiable as insane and hence not legally responsible for criminal acts. It is only
in recent years that the word has been applied to individuals who,
though seriously estranged from the rest of mankind, are not

psychotic. Occasionally, however, the word has been applied to groups that are at odds with some aspect of the society or culture around them—Marx spoke of the alienation of the industrial worker from his labor.

Alienated youths have been vividly portrayed by a number of novelists, notably J. D. Salinger in *Catcher in the Rye* and John Hersey in *Too Far to Walk*. Such novels became popular with large numbers of students who recognized in them something that had meaning to their own situations and their own view of life. The psychological nature of the new alienation has been explored more fully by Kenneth Keniston in *The Uncommitted*, a clinical study of a small group of Harvard undergraduates.[17] Although he chose the more extreme cases for his investigation, Keniston says, "The major themes in the lives of these alienated youths are but extreme reactions to pressures that affect all young Americans . . . the alienated are responding not only to idiosyncrasies of their individual past but to dilemmas of upbringing, to social stress, and to historical losses that affect their entire generation."

Keniston reports that the subjects of his study were "in many respects *too* alienated to be beatniks—a stance which, after all, involves accepting an identity, a sense of solidarity, and a set of expectations about one's 'beat' behavior." And he found few politically active students among his group of alienated. "The quests of most alienated Americans," he says, "are private quests—for personal sentience, for intensified subjectivity, for kicks and stimulation, for individual artistic expression—the alienated express themselves more to achieve self-definition than to persuade others. . . ."

The new alienation, says Keniston, takes the form of "rebellion without a cause, rejection without a program, of refusal without a vision of what should be. . . . Finding out what the alienated are *against* is easy; they excel at scorn, derision, hostility, and contempt, and any statement opposing almost anything will elicit agreement from them provided it is worded in a derisive or scornful way—but finding out what they are *for* is harder . . .

few alienated young men have clear and positive values, readily articulated goals, neatly described life plans. Theirs is an ideology of opposition, and the world offers so many targets for their repudiation that they have little energy left for the development of affirmative values."

Though individuals showing the extreme forms of alienation described by the novelists and Keniston can be found on every campus, their number is so small that they are best dealt with as clinical cases. Of greater concern to the educator is the much larger number of students who show, in lesser degree, some of the traits of alienation, particularly a rejection of adulthood and all that goes with it. Those who are partially alienated choose perpetual adolescence for a variety of reasons, which in some cases clearly includes a neurotic inability to face adult responsibilities, but whatever the reason, they defend and rationalize the choice on the basis of a philosophical conviction that young people have a truer vision of the world and a superior sense of values which are lost when one sells out by becoming a part of the hated "system."

Most of those who reject the adult world find it psychologically necessary to become identified with a subculture made up of others who share their views. During the early sixties the best known of these was that of the beatniks, a subculture that had first come to public attention through the literature of the forties and fifties. Except on a few campuses, the number of students identified with this group was never very large. A considerable number of the "campus beatniks" who got their pictures in the paper were not really students—they were dropouts or nonstudents who lived in pads near a campus because living there was inexpensive and because identification with college students gave them some measure of immunity from the police. In the mid-sixties it was estimated that 3000 such nonstudents lived near the Berkeley campus, where they took part in the demonstrations and protest movements.

In the classroom, student beatniks were rarely troublesome except to professors who were annoyed by unconventional clothing and to other students who resented their air of superiority. Some were widely read, perceptive, and intelligent. Their presence stimulated more conventional students to critical defense of their convictions and added vitality to class discussions. It was their out-of-class behavior that gave the deans of students a bad time.

There is no need to fear that beatniks will ever become the dominant group on campus. Already they are being rapidly replaced by "hippies" and—though the difference may still be unclear to the older generation, a distinction is very important to the hippies, who tell me that beatniks are now considered old-fashioned and really a bit square.

Though the word *beatnik* can be found in Webster's Third ("a person having a predilection for unconventional behavior and dress and often a preoccupation with exotic philosophizing and self-expression"), *hippies* is a newer word that did not come to public consciousness until 1965 or 1966 and has not yet found its way into the dictionaries. It is only vaguely related to the older words *hip*, *hipster*, and *hepster*. Though he often looks like a beatnik to the uninitiated—he is likely to scorn barbershops, beauty parlors, and bathtubs and to wear weird or nondescript clothing—the hippy's philosophy and style of life are somewhat different. Though both groups share the conviction that adults are hypocritical and society corrupt, the hippy is less inclined than the beatnik to be openly bitter about it. He is also less inclined than the demonstrators to demand reforms or to tell adults how to run the world. What he most wants is complete freedom; consequently he is resentful of any effort on the part of parents, college administrators, governmental officials including the police, or any other adults to exercise any kind of control over him.

The hippies profess an encompassing and uncritical love for all mankind. They are quick to defend all criminals, Hell's Angels, even the Nazis. But beneath this protestation of love there often appears to be an underlying hostility, particularly for the "straight" world and for all those in authority. The hippy who forces a flower into the hand of the policeman who arrests him may really be expressing his hostility. And the hippy who professes a love for all mankind may, in the next breath, say that he became a hippy because he hates his parents.

These parents are, in many cases, exemplars of the "straight" world the hippies so emphatically reject. Most of them are politically liberal, well-educated, professional men and women or business executives who have enlightened views of child-rearing, have read Freud and Dr. Spock, and consider themselves permissive. They have given their children all the advantages of upper-middle-class affluence, including the opportunity for a good education.

But the hippy rejects all this, prefers to live very simply, often in a communal pad, and to work only when it is absolutely necessary. He has no interest in a career and seems not to be concerned about the future. In his search for a better life than that of his parents he is likely to quote Thoreau; but he seems not to have read *Walden* very carefully, for instead of living alone in a shack in the wilderness where he can commune with nature the hippy is much more likely to live in the heart of a city where he is surrounded by multitudes and can enjoy such civilized attractions as traffic noise and air pollution. And instead of depending on his own resources for food, clothing, and shelter, as Thoreau did, the hippy is not at all reluctant to accept money from relatives or anyone else who is willing to provide it.

Since the true hippy rejects all status symbols, it is doubtful that any college student who worries about grades and works for a degree can be a true hippy. It would probably be more accurate to say that the college students who call themselves hippies are other-directed individuals, almost pathetically eager to be accepted. They wear nondescript garb and unconventional hair styles for the same reason that a fraternity neophyte wears a tuxedo and accepts a paddling from his "brothers": it is the price of membership.

But the use of LSD is also one of the prices of membership. Were it not for the use of psychedelic drugs, the hippy cult on campus might be regarded as just another passing fad. Beards, beads, and long hair are nothing to worry about—they can be quickly and easily removed when the wearer decides to change his way of life. But there is growing scientific evidence that the effects of the psychedelics may not be so easily eliminated—some evidence, indeed, that LSD may affect changes in the chromosomes that will have a disastrous effect on future generations.

The hippy likes to say that he uses psychedelic drugs because they expand his consciousness and give him a clearer vision of reality. It would be more accurate to say that they heighten his sensations but distort his consciousness and enable him to escape from a reality that he finds unbearable. It is true, of course, that he lives in a troubled world in which there is much hypocrisy, virtue and evil exist side by side, false values are cherished by many, and mankind threatens to destroy itself by bombs, air pollution, or overpopulation. But his sensitive awareness of all this does not adequately explain his decision to reject the world and let others accept the responsibility for improving the lot of mankind while he retreats to his pad to float on a hallucinogenic cloud. The hippy's assumption that he is *more* intelligent and sensitive than other members of his or any other generation is presumptuous. For every hippy on the campus there are two or three other students, equally perceptive, intelligent, sensitive, and well informed, who, though they must live in the same world, are able to face it courageously and willing to work to improve it. The choice of one way of life over another reflects the personality structure of the individual who makes it. In the case of the hippy, the inability to face the world often reflects psychological conflicts dating from childhood or early adolescence. We can sympathize with him, try to understand him, and offer whatever assistance he is willing to accept (usually not very much until he has had a "bad trip" on LSD) without admiring his way of life or holding it up as a model for others to follow.

The picture is thoroughly confused by the fact that a wide variety of students now call themselves hippies. Some of them, instead of rejecting affluence, seem eager to make the most of it.

At vacation time they take jet planes to the beaches of Florida or California and see nothing inconsistent in letting their parents pay the fare. The old-guard hippies of the Haight-Ashbury district of San Francisco (a hippy becomes old guard in about eighteen months) are scornful of this sort of thing and are resentful and disapproving of the thousands of high school youngsters now swarming into the city and calling themselves hippies. The picture of these aging hippies nodding their heads gravely over the antics of youth is one of the more delightful ironies of our time.

If LSD could be eliminated—and I must admit that it is difficult to see how anything so easily concealed can be eradicated by law—it seems probable that the hippy subculture would not last very long. It has no real identity except that which has been given it in popular magazines and no spokesmen compared to the poets and novelists who identified the beatnik culture in the fifties. Allen Ginsberg, who goes from campus to campus at $700 per evening spreading the gospel, is really more a beatnik than a hippy, while Timothy Leary, who gets the same price for advising students to "Turn on, tune in, and drop out," is now so old that today's students consider him faintly ridiculous. The brighter students also are beginning to wonder whether anyone who charges high fees for his speeches is not really a member of the Establishment.

But the use of psychedelic drugs gives the hippy culture an identity that may hold it together and set it apart from the rest of society. Many of the student hippies first used LSD at a high school party, urged on by their friends or dates. Their motivation for the first trip was the same as that which caused their parents and grandparents to try cigarettes and liquor at the same age—the need to be accepted, the desire to taste forbidden fruits, and the excitement of breaking the rules. Since many of today's students live in a world in which there are no effective restrictions on the pleasures of sex and alcohol, there are not many rules left to break, but the use of anything called a drug can be counted on to arouse the ire of parents, college deans, and the police.

Most of the student hippies, provided that they suffer no permanent damage from their use of LSD, probably will become productive members of the community when the attractions of the hippy life begin to pall. Perhaps they will keep their beards —by the time they are middle-aged it is likely that beards will have become a sign of maturity, for it has been noted that beards come and go in cycles of seventy-five to a hundred years and we are about due for a new cycle. During the last half of the nineteenth century beards were worn by several United States Presidents and one was worn by Charles Evans Hughes well into this century. But the next generation of adolescents will establish new youth cults to torment their elders and give themselves some sort of temporary identity and feeling of importance. Meanwhile, the older generation, despite its occasional cries of outrage will, on the whole, be far more tolerant of the young than the young can ever be of their elders—who can lay a better claim to being the misunderstood generation. For while all older people have had the experience of youth with all its anxieties and frustrations, no adolescent has ever known what it is like to be an adult. And no adolescent ever will.

The New Left

Radicalism has always been associated with youth. When Lord Chesterfield said "He who is not a radical at sixteen has no heart" he quickly added "He who is a radical at sixty has no head." When George Bernard Shaw expressed the opinion that anyone under the age of thirty who is not a revolutionist is an inferior, he obviously thought it necessary to place an age limit on the normal revolutionary tendency.

It is both natural and desirable that young people, once they have become aware of the many evils in the world, should fight for causes. It is inevitable that some of those most sensitive to injustice will prefer revolutionary changes to the slower and safer processes of social reform. A radical is merely one whose discontent with the *status quo* is so extreme, and whose impatience is so great, that he is unwilling to work through legal channels even when he lives in a nation whose governmental structure provides for necessary reforms as a part of the democratic process. Usually he is also one who, because he does not yet have an established role in the present system, has little to lose.

Not many of today's college students can legitimately be called radical. The proportion is probably smaller than it was in the thirties and is almost certainly smaller than it is on some of the university campuses of South America and Europe. However small the number of students who can be clearly identified with it, the movement variously called the New Left or the New Radicalism is too significant to be ignored, for it includes the leaders of many of the protest movements and has a recognizable influence on the thinking of many other students. It also has been remarkably successful in making untenable the post of university president.

Most of the available literature on the New Left is in the form of pamphlets, speeches, and articles in minor journals not widely available to the general public. The best book I have seen on the subject is a paperback titled *The New Radicals,* the report of a study sponsored by the Center for the Study of Democratic Institutions.[18] In their introductory chapter, authors Paul Jacobs and Saul Landau say:

> The Movement is a melange of people, mostly young; organizations, mostly new; and ideals, mostly American. In 1960 and 1961 the Freedom Riders and Negro college students who sat-in in the South were acting in the spirit of The Movement. Most of them who protested against President Kennedy's Cuban policy in 1962 were responding to the impulse of the Movement. The same impulse took them south for the Student Nonviolent Coordinating Committee (SNCC) in 1963, got them arrested in Sproul Hall at the University of California in 1964, and marched them to Washington in 1965 to demonstrate their opposition to the war. . . .
>
> To be in The Movement is to search for psychic community, in which one's own identity can be defined, social and

personal relationships based on love can be established and can grow unfettered by the cramping pressures of the careers and life styles so characteristic of America today.

The Movement rejects the careers and life styles of the American liberal, for to The Movement it is the liberal way of life and frame of mind that represent the evil of America. Those in The Movement feel that modern American liberals have substituted empty rhetoric for significant content, obscured the principles of justice by administrative bureaucracy, sacrificed human values for efficiency, and hypocritically justified a brutal attempt to establish American hegemony over the world with sterile anti-Communism. The Movement sees liberals righteously proclaiming faith in American democracy from their comfortable suburban homes or offices, while the United States Air Force drops napalm on villages and poisons the rice paddies.

In their personal life style, their aesthetic sense, many in The Movement reject affluence and its associated symbols. The ambition to escape from poverty is no spur to action in their lives for many are children of America's post-Depression *nouveau* middle class. . . . In some measure, too, the modes of extreme personal behavior adopted by this group—their permissive view of marijuana or hallucinogenics like LSD, their matter-of-fact acceptance of sexual freedom and their habitual profanity —are part of their search for identity. That search assumes a rejection of everything connected with their old identity and of the technological, bureaucratic values they see as dominant in American life.

This New Radicalism of the sixties represents a sharp discontinuity with both the radicalism and the liberalism of previous generations. When the New Left began to emerge the conservative press tended to see it as another Communist front and was delighted to discover that one or two of the student leaders at Berkeley were the sons or daughters of old-time Communists. But though it seems reasonable to suppose that the Communists have made an effort to exploit the movement to their own ends, and though it is true that many of the new radicals prefer the ideologies of Trotsky or Mao to that of Thomas Jefferson, it does not appear that many of the student radicals really are Communists. Most of them have little respect for the present USSR, which they see as just another big impersonal bureaucratic system, and they could not possibly accept the discipline of the Communist party, for they refuse to take orders from anyone.

Older liberals, who recall having been called radicals in their own youth, were at first inclined to defend the new movement. But they were disconcerted to discover that the new radicals are contemptuous of the liberalism of Norman Thomas, Franklin Roosevelt, and Adlai Stevenson, which they regard as soft and ineffective. They were further alarmed to learn that the new radicals do not believe that the democratic process, as represented by the Constitution of the United States, offers much possibility of remedying the evils of the nation.

It would be more accurate to say that the New Left, instead of being either communistic or liberal, is far to the left of both. Ideologically it is anarchistic or nihilistic, for while its members would like to see the destruction of "the system," they have no blueprint for the world of tomorrow. Some of them seem to believe that if "the Establishment" can be overthrown the world will take care of itself without the creation of a new power structure.

Up to now, at least, the members of the New Left have rarely engaged in physical violence, their preference being for nonviolent techniques. But they do not condemn violence when it is perpetrated by individuals or mobs—as when stones are thrown at the police or tomatoes at a speaker. They criticize the use of force only when it is used by the police, the military, or some other arm of the Establishment.

The New Left is much clearer about what it opposes than about what it stands for or hopes to achieve. When I asked a student who had taken part in the Berkeley revolt whether he really believed that Clark Kerr was an evil man or a bad president he replied—with the patient air of one explaining the facts of life to a backward child—"Kerr is an administrator. All administrators, being part of the system, are bad and must go." But when I asked him to describe his ideal university he had nothing to propose. He could only say that he doubted that any university could be anything other than a "factory."

The failure to look ahead and to plan for the future results in part from the fact that the New Left is distinctly a youth movement, made up of adolescents who still feel an extreme hostility toward all the adults who exercise control over them. The only adults whose views are accepted are such writers and speakers as Timothy Leary, Allen Ginsberg, and Paul Goodman who have joined the young in denouncing the older generation.

Because members of the New Left believe that the United States is still a colonial power, led by evil men who are eager to rule the world, they espouse what Irving Howe has described as "a crude, unqualified, anti-Americanism." In any conflict—diplomatic, military, ideological, or economic—between the United States and any other nation they can be counted on to attack U.S. policy, often blindly accepting as truth all the propaganda of our opponents while rejecting as propaganda all statements made by officials of our own government. Their vigorous opposition to our policy in Vietnam is consistent with this view. But the conflict between Israel and the Arab nations in the early summer of 1967 threw them into consternation and caused a serious split within the movement. Some members, remembering the unhappy history of the Jews and their valiant efforts to reestablish a homeland in Israel, thought the U.S. should provide that nation with whatever help it needed, even if it meant going to war. Other members of the New Left reiterated their statements that war is never justified and insisted that what happened in the Near East was none of our affair. This conflict will not easily be resolved, for it brings into focus the basic issue of whether a powerful nation has, or does not have, some responsibility for what happens in the rest of the world.

Most of the members of the New Left reject the rational and intellectual approaches to human problems that have been stressed in the universities of Western nations. Like the beat-niks—and of course some of them are beatniks—they have great faith in emotion and revealed experiences as guides to action and prefer Eastern religions and philosophies such as Zen Buddhism. It is partly because of the rejection of rational approaches that the movement has no clearly stated ideology. Jacobs and Landau say of them: "And while the older ones among them had been able to articulate their views in a speech or pamphlet, some of the younger ones . . . made a virtue of their inability to articulate and analyze coherently. They talked 'from the gut,' stumblingly, haltingly, using the language of the new folksingers, deliberately adopting a style that was the antithesis of what they had learned from their professors."

The New Left is a movement that extends far beyond the campus and includes some groups that have good personal reasons to believe that the nation's problems require drastic solutions. But on the campus at least, the New Left does not appear to be the stuff of which revolutions are made. Revolutions feed upon hun-ger and oppression; most of the college students who identify themselves with the New Left are the overfed, overprotected offspring of affluent parents who have little to gain and much to lose from a revolution. They talk of overthrowing "the Estab-lishment" but have little understanding of what life is like in a revolutionary world in which there is no "system," no "Estab-lishment," no effective government, and no stability. They be-lieve, and with some reason, that drastic solutions are required, but the number of students who are prepared to fight to the death for their beliefs does not appear large enough to threaten the stability of the nation. If there should be a revolution a few students would become deeply involved but others would run for cover, while the great majority would come to the defense of the democratic institutions of the United States.

What Does the Future Hold for Today's Students?

Students now in college were born about the middle of the twentieth century. At the dawn of the twenty-first they will be a part of the generation responsible for the state of the nation and of the world. What will they be like then?

To say that we cannot predict is to say that we know nothing about the process of maturation during the adult years and that we do not know whether their college education and other adolescent experiences will have any lasting effect. To say that they will not differ from preceding generations is to ignore the effects of social change on individual personality. Some things will surely change but in other respects the class of 1970 will, by the year 2000, be much like middle-aged people today.

The years will have taken their toll. Though medical advances cannot be predicted, it seems probable that the majority of both men and women will be peering through their bifocals and taking exercises to reduce their bulging waistlines. If they are not going to the dentist to have their molars replaced with artificial ones it will be because responsible members of the much despised older generation saw to it that the drinking water was fluoridated or because their own parents—who were members of that same older generation—made it possible for them to have good dental care as children.

This generation, like those that have preceded it, will have its failures. Some will become alcoholics or drug addicts; some will be in prison or hospitals for the mentally ill. Many of those who avoid the confining walls will live lives of quiet desperation while they struggle with unresolved personal conflicts. But it seems probable that the majority of those in college today will, by the year 2000, have become responsible members of an adult society, performing their tasks and wondering what to do about the younger generation. They will undergo only a normal amount of frustration and psychological conflict while living lives of great physical comfort and enjoying a considerable amount of leisure.

But what of the conspicuous minorities? Although most of the demonstrators will have been absorbed into the system they now despise, and will be working to improve it, those who have been the leaders of demonstrations may have a more difficult time. Once a leader of protest movements has had his picture in *Life* and *Look* and has had his most extreme views widely quoted in the press he cannot easily retreat to a more moderate position that will make it possible for him to play an effective role in a democratic society. When those of his own age turn against him—as they will—he is likely to become embittered, and as he begins to show signs of age he will find it more difficult to attract youthful followers. At best he can hope to become a speaker at protest meetings, a pamphleteer, or a writer for left-wing publications. At worst he may become a curiosity. But unless things become so bad that a true revolution is a possibility, he is not likely to do much harm.

A few of the alienated and the beat—a very few—will have become great artists, poets, novelists, or musicians: the Ezra Pounds and Gauguins of the new generation. Others will have found their place in society and will discover that their own offspring, who by that time will have founded new youth cults, look upon them with the conviction youth has always had that old folks know nothing about life and inevitably are cautious, stuffy, and conservative. But some of the beatniks and hippies who have not made the transition to maturity will still be struggling desperately to act young and to learn all the eccentricities of a younger generation that will laugh at their efforts.

For those who have rejected maturity and seek perpetual youth the prospects are not bright, because no one remains young very long. The Berkeley rebels who announced loudly "We don't trust anyone over thirty" will find themselves objects of distrust by 1975 and will be hopelessly middle-aged by the year 2000, whether they like it or not.

Some of today's radicals will have executed the classic turn from left to right while others may, by the year 2000, have discovered that the norm has shifted to such an extent that the New Left, or some aspects of it, has become the middle-of-the-road just as the once-radical views of Norman Thomas and the elder La Follette are now incorporated into the platforms of the Democratic and Republican parties. Some of the young radicals will be in Congress, where they will take part in remaking the nation.

But others—particularly the anarchists—will still be far outside the fold. They will have found no place for themselves in a self-governing society and will not have nearly enough followers to enable them to carry out their plans.

On balance, it seems probable that when the present younger generation takes over it will be able to bring about some improvements in the nation and, hopefully, throughout the world. The majority of those within this generation are better educated and better informed than their ancestors. They are more aware of the world that lies outside the United States and beyond the boundaries of Western culture and they have fewer prejudices against "foreigners" and members of other races. A good percentage of them believe deeply in human freedom and are earnestly desirous of improving the lot of mankind. Their prejudice against older people will fade as they become older and their hatred of those in positions of authority will dissipate as they move into positions of authority themselves. Because they have been reared in affluence, they will be less preoccupied with making money than their parents and grandparents and hence can turn their attention to other things.

Whether they can bring an end to the tragedy of war is another matter. They will find, as preceding generations have found, that causes of war are vastly complex, that the decision to eliminate warfare cannot be made unilaterally, and that the machinery for settling international conflicts cannot easily be constructed. But let us hope that when the twenty-first century dawns, they will still be trying.

Though much of the leadership of tomorrow's world must come from those now in college it does not seem likely that it will emerge from the noisy and dissident minorities. Too many of those now making the headlines really are conformists who reveal their essential other-directedness by seizing upon every latest fad of haircut, clothing, slogan, or cause, and who, instead of making their own independent judgments about government policy, the wisdom of using drugs, or the proper uses of sex, merely follow the leader and announce their decisions by wearing buttons bearing slogans written by someone else. Leadership is made of sterner stuff.

If a culture is to retain its vitality and renew itself it must be led by inner-directed men and women who think for themselves and make their own decisions without undue regard for either the ancient traditions or the fads and trends of the moment. Because the pressures to conform, either to the traditional culture or to some bizarre subculture, are very strong, such individuals are rare. The pressures on the young come more from the peer group than from adults—adolescents find it much easier to reject the views of their parents than to reject those of other adolescents. But a youth who cannot stand up against his own peer group is not likely to become a leader of the adult world.

Among today's young people, the greatest potentiality for leadership can be found not among the beatniks, the hippies, or the demonstrators but within the now-silent majority. It will be found in students of strong resolve and high intelligence who, though they are greatly troubled by the state of the world, are willing to wait and get an education before they set out to reform it. These students, though they are aware of the corrupting influence of power, are too wise to believe that all those holding positions of responsibility inevitably are evil. They are too objective to accept the view that wisdom and virtue reside exclusively with either the young or the old; too responsible to respond to the problems of the world by dropping out.

10.   Eros on the Campus

Has There Been a Sexual Revolution?

For as long as I can remember—and my memory for such things goes back into the 1920s—we have been hearing about something called a "sexual revolution." Students of the flapper era, who identified themselves with the "lost generation," dated the revolt from World War I. Undergraduates of the thirties believed that it began with the Depression, when many young people found marriage impossible and consequently looked for other sexual outlets. Those of the fifties thought the sexual revolution was an aftermath of World War II and began when returning veterans encountered patriotic coeds. Today's undergraduates firmly believe that the revolt started about 1960 when they were in junior high and that it somehow is related to both the threat of nuclear war and the invention of the pill.

All these views reveal the innocence of youth, for neither sexual activity nor the open discussion of it is as new as many students believe. In 1721, Harvard students formally debated the question "Whether it be fornication to lye with one's Sweetheart before Marriage." It is unlikely that there has ever been a generation of students to which sex was not a major interest or that did not include many individuals who violated the rules laid down for them by their elders and demanded that the rules be changed.

It requires no great knowledge of history to know that the sexual mores are no more relaxed today than they have been at many other times in man's long past and that the loosening and tightening of the restrictions on sexual activity go in cycles of irregular length that are related to a wide variety of social forces.

The present trend toward a loosening of restraints dates roughly from the beginning of the twentieth century. It is not so much a revolution as a persistent and growing reaction against the restrictive sexual morality that has variously and somewhat carelessly been described as "Puritanical," "Victorian," or "middle-class." The trend was accelerated by the invention of the automobile, improvement in the techniques of birth control, the dislocation of families resulting from the move from farms to cities, and the two world wars that took many young men away from the restraining influences of their home communities. Freer sexual activity was made to seem more necessary by careless reading of Freud and more normal (at least statistically) by careful reading of Kinsey. It both gave rise to and fed upon the literature, motion pictures, and television programs of the twentieth century.

By 1920 students had discovered that a date in an automobile could be something quite different from one in the front parlor with Mother hovering in the background. Their parents were shocked to learn that young people were parking on country roads for purposes other than enjoying the moonlight. But the students who first made this discovery, and now are parents and grandparents, are shocked in turn to learn that students now have dates in dormitory rooms while the Dean of Women looks the other way. Perhaps the activities in either case do not differ greatly from what happened on back porches and in lawn swings in the nineties, but it seems to be generally agreed that the frequency has increased and that a larger proportion of today's adolescents participate freely in what has always been the favorite sport of the human race.

Whatever the change in activity—and no statistics on such a subject can be reliable—there has been a vast change in the kind of advice given to adolescents. A half-century ago the books of intimate advice for boys and girls told readers that any sexual activity outside marriage was sinful, and that premarital activity precluded the possibility of a happy marriage because no man respected a girl who allowed what were then called "liberties." Girls were advised that anything more intimate than handholding aroused the baser passions in a man and could lead to no good.

The books of advice read by teen-agers today are equally moral in their own way but the morality is different. Some sternly advise against all premarital intercourse, but the reasons given are often practical rather than ethical. Nearly all agree that some modest degree of petting and fondling is a normal way of showing deep affection and that such preliminary activities are a necessary prelude to a happy marriage. And every teen-ager has read at least one book in which a psychiatrist, psychologist, or possibly a minister sagely pontificates that while caution is advisable, no activity between two consenting adults is really sinful or necessarily harmful. Any reader over sixteen feels certain that he is an adult and that the consent can be obtained—if necessary with the aid of the book, which can be discussed on the next date.

Students are also aware that many "respectable" adults of this and other centuries, including quite possibly their own parents, have at times violated the conventional codes and seem to be none the worse for it. They have read the biographies of the mistresses of famous men and stories of clandestine affairs between individuals who have played a conspicuous part in history. They are aware of a conspicuous gap between the publicly announced morality and the actual behavior of men and women. Consequently they are not inclined to accept the restrictions that adults attempt to place upon their activities.

The Dilemma

The dilemma faced by young people is clear enough. Males reach their period of greatest sexual vigor and desire at a time preceding marriage, when the doors to socially approved sexual activity are officially closed to them. But these doors, which have never been successfully locked and barred, have now been set aside by a more permissive society. Now that the fears of pregnancy and disease have been substantially reduced, there is even greater need than before for a code of ethics to guide behavior. But, in our pluralistic society, there is no clear-cut moral code for young people to follow.

The dilemma faced by girls is different but no less perplexing. Though some girls of college age have strong sexual urges, most of them are motivated more by the desire to be popular with boys and often by the desire to please one particular boy. They do not want to be considered old-fashioned, moralistic, or stuffy. When they find that other girls among their associates are engaging in sexual activities, and that the boys expect it, they find it difficult to give a socially acceptable reason for refusing.

Many of today's students would like to be conventional and law-abiding, but first they want the conventions and the laws changed to conform to the current practices. They are convinced that the older generation hypocritically gives lip service to a code in which it does not really believe and which it does not always follow. They differ from the students of the twenties and thirties in that while the earlier generation took pleasure in breaking the rules, the new generation demands that the rules be changed. Another difference is that among the older generation, even those who defended premarital sex insisted that it was justifiable only between two individuals deeply committed emotionally to each other, and that it should be of a continuing nature, while some of the college students today hold that neither commitment nor emotional involvement is necessary to sexual enjoyment. The thing to do, they say, is play it cool, avoid involvement, and live for the pleasure of the moment.

It is unlikely that so hedonistic a philosophy will be widely accepted, particularly by girls, most of whom see sex as a step toward a stable family life. Perhaps the younger generation eventually will develop its own code, though by the time it has done so it will probably have become the older generation and will experience the same difficulty older people always have faced in passing their own moral code on to the young.

The New Morality

The new morality, if it is to be acceptable to a substantial majority of the people who are young today, must be one that appeals to people of many religious faiths as well as to those who are indifferent to religion. It must be acceptable to Catholics, Jews, Protestants of many denominations ranging from the Episcopalians to the fundamentalists, as well as to the agnostics and atheists who are found in substantial numbers on today's campuses. It must also be consistent with the knowledge now available from psychology, sociology, anthropology, and biology.

The fact that this seems a large order probably explains why a new morality to replace the old has been so slow in emerging. But unless it does, we are faced with the prospects of moral chaos, for the older sexual morality, based as it was on a combination of religion, tradition, and fears of pregnancy and disease, is not acceptable to most of the people in college today. No student who has studied the sexual practices that prevail in this and other cultures and that have prevailed at different times in history is likely to believe that monogamous marriage is the only outlet for sex that can be defended. He is almost certain to reject the view that all premarital or extramarital sex inevitably leads to guilt feelings, unhappiness, or neurosis. He knows that whether or not one will feel guilty about any kind of behavior depends on what he has been taught and what he has learned from previous experience. He knows that pregnancy can now be prevented by any intelligent adult willing to plan ahead, and he has more confidence than may be justified in his own ability to do the planning.

The view that men want to marry virgins is not nearly so popular with today's college boys as it is with men of lower cultural levels or as it was in Grandfather's day. Girls who know this no longer fear that premarital sexual experience will be a barrier to a happy marriage. No amount of lecturing on the part of older people is likely to change their conviction that some amount of premarital sex is both permissible and quite possibly a necessary prelude to a happy marriage. This does not mean that most of today's young people are or want to be promiscuous. Most of them believe that sex ought to mean something beyond the purely physical and that it ought to be a part of a continuing relationship. But they are convinced that sexual activities involving consenting adults should not be governed by law and that neither college officials nor the police and courts have a moral right to interfere, whatever the law may say. They are determined to bring about a change in the laws and regulations that are inconsistent with their views. And they have a considerable amount of support from older people, including many who are in responsible positions. The laws in England and in several of the United States are already undergoing change in the direction of greater permissiveness. Greater changes will come when those who are now in college reach voting age.

The Kinsey reports revealed that while adolescents, particularly boys, who lack a college education engage in overt sex earlier and more frequently than do those who go to college, the college students of both sexes much more often engage in "heavy petting" which leads to orgasm without actual intercourse. Some writers have said that such petting is the distinctive feature of dating behavior in the present generation, but anyone old enough to remember the flapper era of the twenties will recall that this term was used even then and that it meant just about what it does now. Petting, light or heavy, has been a part of dating behavior for a long time, but it probably is true that there has been a statistical increase in the variety called "heavy" and less moral opposition to it.

Insofar as they draw their conclusions from the printed word, today's students are influenced by the works of Albert Ellis, Kinsey, the Kronhausens, such recent medical reports as those of W. H. Masters and V. E. Johnson, and Hugh Hefner's "*Playboy* philosophy" of recreational sex far more than they are by the now-antiquated views of Havelock Ellis, Krafft-Ebing, Sigmund Freud, and Bertrand Russell. Older people who wish to guide them should be aware of these new sources of enlightenment even though it obviously would be difficult for anyone to devise a workable code of behavior from such an assortment of literary contributions.

Though a new code for sexual conduct clearly is needed, it cannot safely be constructed by adolescents alone; for, as Richard Hettlinger reminds us in *Living with Sex*: "There is no field of human activity in which it is so easy to deceive oneself and to be convinced by arguments which are in fact nothing but rationalizations of clamant desires." [19] In planning the new morality, young people will need all the advice they can get from older people whose desires presumably have cooled a bit and who can take a longer view. But, being young, they are not likely to take it.

The new code must be based upon a clear recognition of the fact that most educated and enlightened people of all ages look upon sexual desire as biologically, socially, and psychologically normal rather than as something evil, dirty, or shameful. They reject as ridiculous the view that the desire to produce offspring is the only legitimate motivation for sexual activities. Because they accept adolescent petting as normal and know that sex takes many forms, they place less emphasis than their ancestors on the importance of technical virginity. They are aware that sexual desire is strong in youth and that efforts to postpone sexual activities until marriage are at best futile and perhaps both unnecessary and undesirable.

But there is no agreement on what the new code should be, for there is a solid nucleus of more conservative people on every college campus, and a still larger number off campus, who think that it is essential that we preserve some aspects of the traditional morality. Students holding such views and living up to the older code can be found even on the campuses reputed to be most liberal in their attitudes; a Reed professor recently was quoted as saying "There's a lot more virginity around here than you might expect."

One thing seems clear: the new code, to be acceptable, must grant equal freedom to both sexes even though it still is true that it is the girls who have the babies. Throughout the eighteenth and nineteenth centuries it was customary for college boys to have their first sexual experience with "town girls" or prostitutes and then look for virgins of their own social class to marry. Co-education has changed that. Today most of the college boys who have premarital sex have it with girls of their own social and educational level, often with the girls they eventually marry. The double standard is no longer acceptable to either sex.

Early marriage, when it is combined with early parenthood, seems to create as many problems as it solves; the divorce rate among those who marry in their teens is substantially higher than among those who marry later. But it might be possible to provide for a new kind of temporary marriage that would enable young couples to live together during their college years without subterfuge or hypocrisy and would provide a legitimate outlet for sexual urges without all the responsibilities of conventional marriage.

Forty years ago, Judge Ben Lindsey of the juvenile courts of Denver proposed what he called "Companionate Marriage" whereby young couples might legally live together for a time with the understanding that divorce could be obtained by mutual consent so long as there were no children. The world was not ready for so drastic a solution; though Lindsey's plan was applauded by some it was roundly condemned by many and led to no action. But when Margaret Mead recently suggested a somewhat similar plan she met with much less opposition. Perhaps the nation is almost ready to accept such an arrangement, but it will surely take several decades to get the necessary laws through the state legislatures. In any case a good many of today's young people want a greater degree of freedom to experiment than would be provided for by any form of monogamous marriage.

Unless some solution is found we shall undoubtedly see a continued relaxation of standards, a growing contempt for the traditional rules and laws governing sexual activities, and still more confusion on the part of young people as to what is and what is not acceptable. If our society takes a downward trend, historians and archeologists of the future who dig up the remnants of our culture will probably conclude that a decline of sexual morality was a major cause of the deterioration. But if the culture continues to survive and flourish despite a greater degree of sexual freedom, tomorrow's historians will call attention to the fact that sexual freedom has been a characteristic of many of the greatest periods of human achievement. And they will find many examples to cite.

PART THREE
THE ACADEMIC LIFE

11. The Crumbling Ivory Tower

Throughout the nineteenth century and well into the twentieth, a man or woman who chose to make a career of teaching in an undergraduate college could look forward to a quiet life, probably in a small town, with time for leisurely reading and quiet contemplation. His duties, in addition to teaching two or three hours a day, would include grading papers, holding conferences with students, participating in faculty committees, and occasionally supervising student activities. But he would not be expected to give much time to research or writing, except possibly during his free summers, and there were no federally sponsored projects to be administered because no one had yet dreamed of using federal funds for such purposes. He could look forward to long vacations and a five-day week at a time most people worked fifty weeks a year and six days a week. Though his income would be modest, he could probably manage to take one or two trips to Europe during his lifetime. For those of the proper temperament, it was a good life.

These professors of a bygone day were expected to select a discipline or a group of related disciplines but they were not narrowly specialized. In the smaller colleges a single professor might teach several of the natural sciences. It was not unusual for the same professor to teach philosophy, psychology, and education. The history teacher taught both American and European history, the English teacher both English and American literature, and the classicist both Latin and Greek. The college professor of those days was rarely a distinguished scholar but was often a man of broad intellectual interests.

The young man who sets out to be a professor today can anticipate a very different life. His work will be much more highly specialized, he will spend less time with students, and he will be under greater pressure to engage in productive scholarship at a time when it is becoming increasingly difficult to find an outlet for publication. His salary will be higher but he will have less time to enjoy its benefits. He is much more likely than his predecessors to find it necessary to work in a large city and to become a commuter, for the most rapidly growing colleges are located in urban centers.

The change began with the introduction of the Germanic university tradition during the last three decades of the nineteenth century. Most of the smaller colleges were not immediately affected, but those that became universities underwent dramatic change. In the university tradition a professor was expected to be a productive scholar who devoted much of his time to research and writing. In order to conform to the traditions of scholarship he found it necessary to select a narrow specialty: the Italian Renaissance, Chaucer, the anatomy of vertebrates, or the Civil War. As he became more careful and meticulous as a scholar he became less interesting as a person, because of the narrowness of his interests. He also became less able to communicate with those outside his specialty, and consequently less effective as a teacher of undergraduates. Whenever possible he solved this problem for himself by avoiding undergraduate teaching and giving his attention to graduate students interested in his own specialty. When these graduate students took jobs as college teachers, they were eager to continue in the university tradition. They demanded the right to teach their own specialties, with the result that many new and highly specialized courses were introduced into the undergraduate curriculum. The college became more like a graduate school even though its announced aims, and the goals of its students, were different. Much of the pressure for research and publication came not from administrators or from lay boards but from professors steeped in the university tradition.

Beginning in the thirties, another change occurred in the academic life. Professors were called to Washington by President Roosevelt to advise and take part in the New Deal. At first only the faculties of Harvard, Columbia, and a few other major universities were affected, but during the forties and fifties more and more college professors from all kinds of colleges and universities were called upon to advise the federal and state and local governments. The trend gained impetus in the sixties when President Kennedy drafted Harvard professors to help him advance the New Frontier and later when President Johnson began to look beyond Harvard for academic advisers familiar with other parts of the nation. But the seduction of professors from the campus cannot be fully explained by the preference of these three Presidents for advisers with academic backgrounds. Industry, too, has become dependent upon the academic community for much of its top-level talent.

Today any professor of note is likely to spend a substantial part of his time off-campus as a consultant to something or other. Some have joined the jet set and travel all over the world on expense accounts. This adds to the prestige of the college or university and broadens the horizons of the professor, but it also causes him to give less of his time and attention to teaching.

Moreover, many of the professors who stay on the campus have become the administrators of projects involving research grants from foundations or the federal government. The administrator of a project is too busy supervising the work of researchers, graduate students, and secretaries to spend much time in the classroom. It can no longer even be said that a professor is a man who "never met a payroll," for the directors of projects find it necessary to spend much of their time knocking on the doors of foundation officials, private grantors, and federal bureaucrats to get the funds to pay their assistants.

A half-century ago the common criticism that professors lived in ivory towers, isolated from the realities of the world around them, had some basis in fact. Often the walls were so high that professors were unaware of the criticism, but those who heard it replied that the tower was a necessary protection in order that a scholar might be free to contemplate and to pursue his scholarly activities. Now that protection has been lost. Today if you want to find a man or woman who has read widely in many fields, and has had ample time to think about what he has read, the campus is a poor place to look.

These changes are understandable in terms of the pressures and social changes that have brought them about. Professors cannot be blamed for adapting themselves and their work to a changing world in which the status symbols have shifted. But the effect on undergraduate liberal education has been disastrous, particularly in the large universities which get most of the research grants and whose professors are most likely to be seduced away from the job of teaching.

Opportunities and Prospects

Our institutions of higher learning now employ some 400,000 faculty members on a full- or part-time basis. The number will pass the half-million mark soon after 1970 and is expected to reach 600,000 or 700,000 by 1980. Most of these individuals, though they spend part of their time in the classroom, do not like to be called teachers—they prefer to be identified as historians, philosophers, physicists, chemists, biologists, psychologists, anthropologists, sociologists, economists, political scientists, educators, classicists, or mathematicians. In the college catalogue about one-fourth of them are listed as "professors," half are either "associate professors" or "assistant professors," while the others are "lecturers," "instructors," or "teaching assistants." A few are designated "research professors" or "distinguished service professors."

To an outsider, these titles can be confusing. An assistant professor does not assist anyone, lecturers do no more lecturing than those in other ranks, instructors are not the only ones who instruct, and research professors are not the only ones who do research. Instructors usually are young men or women just getting started; teaching assistants are graduate students who handle discussion sections; while a lecturer may be a noted scholar who prefers not to accept the full responsibilities of a faculty member.

In many institutions only the two top ranks are granted tenure and only the three professorial ranks are counted as faculty. Within these three ranks there is not much differentiation of duties. All do some teaching, accept committee responsibilities, and, in most institutions, are expected to spend some time in research or other scholarly work. A professor, sometimes called a "full professor" to distinguish him from those whose titles carry the adjectives *associate* or *assistant*, draws a higher salary, usually has more choice of the subjects he will teach, and may be able to avoid eight-o'clock classes, but his workload and responsibilities do not differ greatly from those of assistant and associate professors.

If the Ph.D. is what it has often been called—the union card for college teaching—it must be said that professors have a very weak union, for only about 40 per cent of all college teachers hold any kind of doctoral degree. Most of the others, however, have done some work beyond the master's and many have completed all the requirements for the doctorate except the dissertation and final oral examination. The percentage of doctorates is highest in the graduate schools, where nearly all faculty members hold the degree. It is lowest in the denominational colleges and in the junior colleges. In the better state colleges and the more affluent independent colleges the number of doctorates is typically 40 per cent to 60 per cent of the faculty. But doctorates are most highly prized and most greatly stressed in the upwardly mobile institutions such as colleges eager to become universities. Some of the older and more self-confident institutions do not even bother to list degrees in the catalogue. It is notable, too, that the title *Doctor* is heard much more frequently in the upwardly striving institutions than in the prestigious ones where the title *Mister* is more common even for senior professors. And a noted scholar who lacks the doctorate is more likely to get a professorship at Harvard or Chicago than at a weaker university that is still trying to impress the accrediting agencies.

A college or university teacher of whatever rank spends much less time in the classroom than does an elementary or high school teacher. In most institutions, those who teach undergraduates spend from ten to fifteen hours per week in class, the larger number being more typical in junior colleges than in four-year institutions. Those who teach graduate and professional students in universities have lighter teaching assignments—usually six to eight hours and sometimes less if the institution places great emphasis on research. Some "research professors" do no classroom teaching, though most of them work on an individual basis with a few doctoral candidates.

In spite of teaching loads that appear light to a public school teacher, nearly all college teachers believe that they are overworked. It is probably true that most of them devote more hours per week to their work than do most people today except business executives and the members of other learned professions. Their work, in addition to teaching, consists of preparing lectures, grading papers, library reading, committee work, research, and writing. Many of them also spend time in consultation with individual students. For some who are highly motivated, this adds up to a very heavy load. But at the other extreme are a considerable number of college professors who do no research or writing, give the same lectures year after year or filibuster in class with no planned discourse, see students as rarely as possible, and grade papers hurriedly and carelessly. Since the students on almost every campus are aware of the existence of some such professors, it would be futile to deny that they exist. For an individual lacking in motivation, college teaching *can* be a soft job once he has acquired tenure. But for most it is not.

Salaries

Academic salaries depend both upon the institution and the individual's academic rank. Though high salaries are correlated with institutional prestige, there are some very sharp exceptions —the two institutions paying the highest median salaries in 1966 were Harvard and Parsons, only one of which appears on the lists of prestige institutions. The lowest salaries are found in the weaker denominational college, but some church-related schools pay salaries above the national average. Most state colleges and universities fall in the middle salary groups, though some of them offer high salaries to a few individuals.

Formal salary scales are more common in state institutions than in private ones, where many administrators prefer to keep salaries a secret and to negotiate individually with each faculty member. On a typical scale the salary of full professors is about twice that of an instructor—the range from bottom to the top of the scale is not nearly as great as the range in industrial management, where high-ranking officers often draw from five to ten times as much as junior executives. The usual effect of establishing a rigid salary scale is to raise the salary in the lower ranks and to lower the top. Consequently the more distinguished scholars are likely to find their way to institutions that determine salaries on an individual basis and are prepared to pay what the market demands.

In a day of rising salaries any figures that can be offered in a book are likely to be obsolete before they are read. It is possible, however, to offer some information about the past and make some predictions about the future.

The typical professor who is now approaching the end of his career (for "typical" substitute *average, middle-grade, moderately successful,* or the statistical term *modal* if you prefer) became an instructor in a college around 1930 at a salary of not more than $1800 or $2000. After teaching for a few years he returned to the university to get his Ph.D., but because promotions were slow during the Depression, he did not become an assistant professor, with a salary of perhaps $3000, until about 1940. Unless he entered the armed forces he became an associate professor during the forties at a salary of about $4000. During the fifties he finally achieved his professorship, by which time salaries had risen sufficiently to bring his to $8000 or $9000. Today he draws $13,000 or $14,000 and expects to receive an increase of about 6 per cent a year until his retirement, after which his retirement pay will be about half his terminal salary. Though he engages occasionally in ritualistic complaint about the low salaries of the academic world, his secret conviction is that he has done rather well financially, even though a good part of the increase has been offset by inflation. He is certainly living better than he ever expected when he was a graduate student. But he probably is not living as well as professors did in 1900, when those at Harvard were getting $4000, those at Johns Hopkins $5000, and those at Columbia $5000 to $7500.[20] Such salaries were probably five times as much as the incomes of men employed in the skilled trades at that time. Today the average professor makes only about twice as much as a truck driver or plumber, but he does not live in poverty.

The young man who enters the academic life today, if he has a Ph.D. and was a teaching assistant in graduate school, will probably skip the instructor rank. In his first full-time job he will be an assistant professor with a salary between $8000 and $10,000 if he is employed by a moderately prosperous institution. By the time he is thirty-five, he can reasonably expect to be an associate professor drawing at least $13,000. Sometime in his early forties he will become a professor with a salary which, by 1980, may be anywhere between $20,000 or $30,000 if salaries continue to rise at the current rate. This, of course, assumes continued affluence and moderate inflation—if there should be a depression these figures will be reduced but the professor's buying power may still rise, as did that of most academic men during the Depression of the thirties. Once he has achieved tenure, a professor is not likely to lose his job even during a severe depression unless he is in a borderline institution that is forced to close.

In the mid-sixties only the top 5 per cent of full professors (slightly more than 1 per cent of *all* faculty members) drew salaries of $20,000 or more for nine months. Most of these individuals taught in graduate and professional schools, but some were scattered among a wide variety of other institutions. These relatively affluent professors were also the ones most likely to have substantial additional income from speeches, consulting fees, and royalties. I could name at least a dozen professors whose royalties from textbooks bring them $50,000 or more a year; there probably are a great many more in the nation but no one except the Internal Revenue Service has a record of their outside earnings. Obviously it is possible for the more fortunate academic men to have good incomes without deserting the academic world.

Deans and presidents make more than professors but not enough more to make the affluent professors want to become administrators. Administrative salaries are usually for eleven or twelve months and hence are not really comparable with those of professors, whose basic salary is for nine months and who get an additional stipend if they teach during the summer term.

In 1965–1966 the mean salary of undergraduate deans was $15,703, while the mean for those in large universities was about $20,000. Only a few made as much as $30,000. In the same year the median salary of all college and university presidents was $19,638,[21] but the median for those in large universities was about $30,000. One president received $55,000 while seventeen others received $40,000 or more. But at the other extreme were about twenty-five presidents of small denominational colleges who made less than $10,000. It is obvious that administrative salaries in colleges and universities are far below those of officers in business and industry who carry comparable responsibility, but they do not differ greatly from those of state and federal officials of high rank. Indeed it is not unusual for the president of a state university to receive a salary higher than that of the governor of the same state.

One of the attractive features of the academic life is the freedom of movement it offers. Members of the fee-taking professions rarely enjoy such mobility. A physician or lawyer, once he has established his practice, cannot move without serious financial loss. A government employee must live where the job is. A corporation executive must go where the corporation sends him. Many a man who would like to live in a small town, in California, or in a smaller city, must live in New York, Chicago, or Boston because his job exists only there. Others who would like to live in Manhattan must remain in a small town.

An academic man, in contrast, can choose his place of residence without significant loss of professional opportunity or income. When he receives his Ph.D. he will probably have a choice of jobs in large cities, small cities, and small towns, in New England, New York, the Deep South, the Middle West, the Far West, or even in Hawaii or Alaska. He can choose to be a part of an institution with 100,000 students or of one of 500 students. And whether he chooses an assistant professorship in Manhattan; Berkeley; Northfield, Minnesota; Amherst, Connecticut; Wooster, Ohio; Nashville, Tennessee; or Bellingham, Washington, his starting salary will fall within a narrow range—as of 1968 probably between $8000 and $10,000—not enough difference to pay for the difference in cost of living between one part of the country and another.

If he does not find a job in exactly the place he wants at the time of getting his degree, the academic man can move after a year or two with no loss of status or salary. It is not unusual for a man with a Ph.D. to begin his teaching as an instructor in a university in New England, move on after a year or two to an assistant professorship in a Big Ten University, then to an associate professorship in a small liberal arts college, and then eventually settle down as a professor in a large state college on the West Coast. And each time he moves he will get an increase in salary and a raise in rank. But if he finds a place he likes anywhere along the way he may stay there, and if he demonstrates his competence he has a good chance of promotion to a tenured position in which he may remain until retirement.

After he has decided upon the kind and size of institution the academic man may choose the kind and size of community in which he wants his family to live. Both New York University and the University of Illinois are large and complex institutions with graduate and professional schools, but one is located in Greenwich Village while the other is on the prairies surrounded by fields of waving corn. Both Swarthmore and Carleton are prestigious small colleges that admit only academically talented students, but one is located on the outskirts of the City of Brotherly Love while the other is in a village of 4000 famous for being the site of a Jesse James bank robbery. San Francisco State and Bowling Green State are large state institutions that grew out of normal schools, but one is in a prosperous farming community while the other is in the home of the hippies and the topless go-go girls. Both Yale and Dartmouth are Ivy League institutions, but one is surrounded by the smog of New Haven while the other is in the ski country. The academic man who has demonstrated his competence can take his choice.

Of course no individual receives offers from so wide a range of institutions, but the jobs are there for those who plan ahead and make the most of their opportunities. Some limitations on easy movement are established by the academic pecking order. It is easier to move from Princeton to Podunk than from Podunk to Princeton—always easier to move down the totem pole (though often with a higher rank and salary) than to move up. It is easier to move west than east because the western colleges and universities are expanding more rapidly—California institutions persistently raid the colleges of the East and Middle West. Two-thirds of the faculty in my own college in Bellingham, Washington are from the East. But some of the former students of this college now teach at Yale, M.I.T., Swarthmore, and other eastern institutions. Mobility in both directions is possible and the opportunity adds zest to the academic life.

The Professor's Three Roles

An academic man of whatever rank is expected to play three roles: he is a teacher, a scholar, and a faculty member. As a teacher his responsibility is to his students, as a scholar to the world of scholarship and specifically to that segment he has chosen as his discipline, as a faculty member to the college or university that employs him. The conflict among these roles is a major source of tension in the academic life.

It is difficult for any individual to play all three roles well even if he has all the varied talents required; time does not permit it.

He must choose, and though he ought to make the choice when he selects the institution in which he will work, many professors fail to do so and find themselves in institutions that expect something other than what they have to offer.

In the graduate school of a university the professor's first responsibility is to the advancement of scholarly knowledge. No individual who is unwilling to devote a substantial portion of his energies to research or other scholarly work is likely to be happy in such an institution, for he will find himself under constant pressure to publish. But in many American universities, the university professor is also expected to spend a part of his time teaching undergraduates. If he teaches badly the student will have good reason to complain and the professor is likely to be irritated and frustrated. If he teaches well the teaching will take time he might prefer to spend in research.

In an undergraduate college, the professor's responsibility to his students has traditionally come first. It ought to come first. Today, however, a growing number of colleges, in their effort to gain status by becoming more like universities, require publication as a basis for promotion. The rationalization used to justify this requirement, even for teachers of freshmen and sophomores, is that a professor who does not publish is not "keeping up with his field"—a dubious assumption that I shall examine more fully in a later chapter. But even if the young faculty member is teaching in a college that does not require publication, he knows he must spend a part of his time in scholarly research if he wishes at some later time in his career to move to a university.

As a faculty member, the academic man in either a college or a university is expected to contribute to his institution by participating in faculty committees, advising student organizations, helping plan new buildings, advising the board of trustees on the selection of a new president when that office is open, taking part in planning the curriculum, and in many other ways. If the faculty refuses to accept such responsibilities the administration becomes excessively powerful and professors become mere employees instead of integral parts of their institutions. But such faculty responsibilities take a great deal of time and reduce the amount of time available for teaching and research.

The graduate programs that lead to the Ph. D. degree prepare individuals specifically for only one of these three responsibilities—research. Any Ph.D. knows how to follow a line of scholarly investigation and how to publish his results. Whether he knows how to teach is less certain. It can be assumed that he has acquired a fund of scholarly knowledge in a discipline and that he has some degree of familiarity with the sources of knowledge in his field, but it is less than certain that he will know how to transmit his knowledge to students by proposing problems that will arouse their interest in order that they may learn. On the day he receives his Ph.D. he is better prepared to teach a graduate course in the limited areas he chose for his own dissertation than to teach a freshman course designed to introduce students to his discipline. He is almost certainly not prepared to teach interdisciplinary courses of the kind taught in many undergraduate colleges. Only a few graduate schools have remedied this defect by requiring candidates for the Ph.D. to teach undergraduates under supervision before the degree is granted, even though more than half those who receive the degree become teachers of undergraduates. Consequently, a large proportion of the young men and women with Ph.D. degrees do their best to avoid teaching courses for freshmen and sophomores. They teach such courses under duress and hence without much enthusiasm. And the students know.

Many graduate schools make no effort whatever to prepare future college teachers for their role as faculty members who will take part in institutional policy-making. Many young graduates scarcely know the difference between a college and a university and know little or nothing about the history of academic institutions. Many are unaware of the rights and responsibilities of students, faculty members, administrators, or boards of regents. When conflicts break out they are unprepared, because of this ignorance, to act wisely or to take effective part in solving the problems.

A few universities now offer one or two elective courses in higher education for future college teachers. But the great majority of the men and women who become college teachers enter the academic life prepared for only one of their three roles. If they are ever to become effective teachers of undergraduates or competent members of the policy-making body called a faculty, they must learn on the job. Fortunately many do. Unfortunately many do not, and their failure is a major problem to institutions of higher learning.

12. Portrait of the Professor

Professors, even more than other people, dislike being stereotyped. When a writer or speaker attempts to make generalizations about them they are likely to protest that no generalizations are possible because they are all individuals and individualists. Though they do not doubt that policemen have a "police mentality" and generals a "military mind," they deny that there can be such a thing as an "academic personality."

It is true that professors come in all sizes and shapes and from all social groups. Their political views cover the full range from the extreme left to the extreme right, though the central tendency is to the left of center. Their religious convictions range from orthodoxy to atheism. Some are ascetic while others, in the words of George Jean Nathan, are "pretty glandular boys." Their IQs range from only slightly above average to the very top of the scale. They dress in styles ranging from that of Madison Avenue to that of beatniks, range in age from the early twenties to the eighties, and are of at least two sexes.

But the fact remains that the average or modal professor differs substantially from the typical businessman, skilled laborer, farmer, politician, actor, or physician. And the differences are worth noting because the kind of education offered by a college or university depends in large part on the characteristics of individual faculty members. No matter what the catalogue may say, no matter what the presidents and deans may announce, once a professor has walked into his classroom and closed the door he teaches just about what and as he pleases. Consequently it becomes important to know what pleases him and what his biases are.

The professor's view of the world has been molded by the fact that he has spent a very long time as student and faculty member in institutions of higher learning—a very special environment. It is not the ivory tower that outsiders suppose it to be. It is rarely a place of leisure, and it has its share of rugged competition. But it is different, for in this environment the things most prized differ substantially from the values that hold sway in the business world or the fee-taking professions such as medicine and law.

In the academic world, money is sought as a necessary convenience, but its possession has very little to do with establishing an individual's status. Conspicuous consumption has a negative effect on status—the professor who buys a Cadillac gets more disapproval than approval from his colleagues who are convinced that Cadillacs are for business executives, prize fighters, movie stars, and surgeons—not for intellectuals. And when he travels by ship or plane the professor is likely to go tourist even if he can well afford a first-class passage.

The academic man does not fit neatly into the American structure of social classes as described by sociologists. His income would place him in the middle class; his education would entitle him to a higher status; but he may live in a part of town occupied by almost any class. In his home the kitchen and bathroom are similar to those of any middle-class home, but the living room displays more books, records, and original paintings than does the living room of a businessman with a similar income. The furniture is likely to be a bit shabbier, modern, or a bit unusual; rarely is it very expensive. In his office, a professor almost never displays his diplomas on the walls—a practice that is standard with dentists, physicians, and morticians. And when he signs his letters he is not likely to place *Ph.D.* or any other degree after his name unless the degree was very recently acquired.

When I enter the lobby of a New York hotel full of conventioneers I find it interesting to try to guess the nature of the group before peering surreptitiously at one of the badges to verify my guesses. Although the differences between groups of academic men and those attending other conventions are subtle and my judgment of them essentially a clinical one, I find that I rarely mistake a collection of philosophers, psychologists, mathematicians, or historians for one of businessmen or men of other professions. If the men are uniformly dressed and if they greet each other with a firm handshake and a straight look in the eye they are likely to be junior executives or middle-management types rather than professors. If they are expensively dressed and a bit pompous they are likely to be physicians. But if they come in much greater variety, if some are extrovert and a bit manic while others are somewhat shy and diffident, and many are carelessly dressed or wearing the tweeds rarely seen in a hotel lobby, they are probably academic men. (College presidents pose a special problem, for they are likely to look and act more like business executives than professors.)

It is indeed true that academic men are less likely to conform to a pattern than men in other vocations. They have less need than lawyers, salesmen, or advertising men to make a good first impression because they deal with the same colleagues and students for many months at a time. They are employed on the basis of their academic records, publications, past accomplishments, and recommendations rather than on the basis of interviews where clothing, attitudes, and address can be evaluated by a stranger. And they live in a world in which individuality is not only permitted but encouraged.

Most academic men are relatively free of racial and religious bias and take a liberal position on civil rights. But the professor is likely to have his own biases that make him eager to establish a pecking order of disciplines and institutions with his own at the top. If his field is physics or chemistry, he thinks it a bit presumptuous of psychologists and sociologists to call themselves scientists. If he works in a pure science he feels quietly superior to those who must teach the practical applications. If he is a classicist he is likely to be convinced that the decline of higher education began when Latin and Greek were dropped from the requirements for graduation. And if he teaches any academic subject there is a good chance that he can see no legitimate place for professors of education on a college faculty. In most cases he is too much of a gentleman to state his biases publicly, but these convictions lie at the root of many conflicts within the faculty and make the construction of a curriculum more difficult.

Unless he has moved around a good bit he is likely to have a number of geographic and institutional biases. If his entire experience has been in New England he is apt to doubt that the higher learning is possible west of the Hudson. If he teaches on either the Atlantic or the Pacific coast he finds it difficult to believe that there are any good colleges in Kansas. If his entire experience has been in private colleges and universities, he is likely to believe that state colleges enroll only slow learners. If he teaches in a small liberal arts college he probably shudders at the impersonality of multiversities. And if he teaches in a large university he soon becomes convinced that higher education requires a cyclotron and a library of at least two or three million volumes.

The peculiar biases of the professor result in part from the nature of graduate education and in part from his subsequent experiences. The training and subtle indoctrination of a candidate for the Ph.D. give him confidence in the road to truth pursued in his own discipline while making him skeptical of the approaches used in others. It is difficult for a scientist to believe that the humanistic approaches to truth have any real validity, equally difficult for the humanistic scholar to believe that science can deal effectively with the things that matter most. This is the basis for the split between the two academic cultures on which C. P. Snow has commented.

After he receives his doctorate, the academic man faces a captive audience that has little opportunity to challenge his views, particularly if he teaches large lecture sections in a university in which graduate students handle the discussion sections. If he writes only for journals within his own discipline, his convictions about the importance of that discipline and the relative insignificance of others are not likely to be challenged by anyone.

The professor's individuality is made possible by the fact that the necessary traditions of academic freedom and job security make it possible for him to display idiosyncrasies that could quickly end the career of a salesman, military officer, minister, or business executive. Once he has acquired tenure he enjoys a degree of freedom denied most contemporary men in positions of comparable prestige—a fact of which he is rarely aware until he moves to an administrative position or accepts a job in industry or government, but one that substantially influences his style of life and the development of his personality.

13. The Not-so-private World of Administrators

Administrative office is not the normal goal of an academic man. The young instructor, when he dreams about the future, does not envision himself in the president's office meeting deans, alumni, parents, legislators, or potential donors. Though he is no less eager for higher status, greater rewards, and expanded opportunities than are men in other fields, his goals preclude the acceptance of administrative responsibility. If his ambitions are high, his dream is to become a great scholar or scientist whose publications will be widely quoted in the learned journals. He would like to win a Nobel Prize or write a book that will survive the centuries. At the very least he would like to add a few substantial bricks to the edifice of scholarship. Only after this dream has become a reality—or when it has begun to fade—do his thoughts turn to the possibility of accepting an administrative position.

Even then he may be reluctant. Though he feels it an honor to be offered an administrative post in his college and would like to have the extra money, a better office, and a full-time secretary, he knows that administration will be a new way of life for which he is not emotionally prepared. The professor who becomes a dean or president is not merely taking a step upward, like the colonel who becomes a general or the junior executive who becomes a vice-president—he is changing vocations and turning his back on the world he knows best and for which he feels best qualified. He is entering a new world for which his formal education did not prepare him.

When a professor becomes a dean or president, the contemplative life of the scholar—to which he has always aspired, though he probably has never quite achieved it—is gone forever. Now he is a public figure who must make frequent ceremonial appearances, attend numerous banquets, and make speeches not only to students and faculty but to alumni, legislators, and the local Rotary Club. He must learn to guard his statements, for his slightest blunder or slip of speech will be discussed, and his statements will be widely quoted and misquoted. His private life becomes an open book and his social life is altered. No longer can he invite a few friends in to dinner without thought to the feelings of those not invited. And once the step is taken it is difficult to turn back, for a president or dean cannot easily return to a professorship, even though he may still hold the title.

But there are compensations, including higher salaries, expanded opportunities for public service, and greater prestige outside the academic community. Consequently, a considerable number of academic men decide sooner or later to become candidates for administrative office. It is fortunate that they do because there are never enough competent men available to fill the 200 college presidencies and much larger number of deanships that fall vacant each year within the United States. Most of these must be filled by professors because the success of candidates brought in from outside the academic community has not, with some rare exceptions, been high. Academia is a different world and the man who is already mature when he enters it has much to learn and too little time to learn it. If he attempts to apply principles he has learned in the world of business, government, or the military establishment, he soon antagonizes both students and faculty and often makes himself ridiculous.

The ideal candidate for high administrative office in the academic world is a scholar who is competent in his academic discipline but has outgrown it. He has the badges of respectability, including a Ph.D. and a list of publications in scholarly journals, but has decided that there must be something more to life than being a chemist, mathematician, or historian. He is interested in the total education of students and the entire world of scholarship. Like most academic men he has always been dissatisfied with the way colleges are run and feels he is ready to do something about it.

Many competent academic men come to such conclusions soon after they achieve their professorships. The urge to carry on research has subsided somewhat and they find classroom work less satisfying than once it was. The man who becomes a full professor in his late thirties or early forties knows he faces another twenty-five or thirty years with no opportunity for further promotion or for an enlargement of responsibility unless he still has some hope of becoming a great scholar. And he knows that unless he is well on the road to greatness by the time he is forty he is unlikely ever to achieve it. The prospect of being a professor for the rest of his life is not quite enough. For some, administrative work seems the answer.

The traditional first step is to become chairman of a department. This does not remove him from his discipline, but if the department is a large one the chairman soon discovers that the time available to him for teaching, research, and writing has been sharply curtailed by the new demands on his time. He must spend many hours working with committees on curricular matters, with secretaries on problems of scheduling, reconciling conflicts within his department, and recruiting new members for it. He has become an administrator whether he likes it or not.

A department chairman, if he is outstandingly successful, becomes a potential candidate for a deanship when that post falls vacant or when some other college is looking for a dean. But for an academic man it is a much larger step because it means breaking ties with his own departmental discipline that have been firm since graduate-school days. The dean must represent the college or the scholarly world rather than a single subject and must lean over backward not to make special concessions based upon loyalty to his own field.

The dean, if his success is conspicuous, becomes a potential candidate for a presidency. By this time he may be committed to a career in administration and eager to get on with it—he may have concluded that if one is to be an administrator he may as well be top man and have more assistants to take care of the details. Still he is aware of the greater public nature of the presidency and may not be quite sure that this is what he wants.

Authors of campus novels tend to construct plots based upon a battle for the presidency between two ambitious men who are determined to get the job at all costs. In real life such conflicts are rare. Often the best candidate is ambivalent about the job, particularly if he is a noted scholar torn between his responsibility to his discipline and his duty to the college or university. Frequently he is not at all eager to compete for the presidency and must be persuaded to accept it.

Those who do accept often have regrets when they become aware of the heavy load of responsibilities, including the many ceremonial duties that seem trivial but cannot be escaped. Some are alarmed to discover how little security is inherent in the top administrative post; many are troubled to learn how little real influence a president has over the dissident faculty members or students who want to test the limits of administrative authority.

No one should accept a college or university presidency unless he is willing to live dangerously. Unlike the tenured professor, who in most institutions can be discharged only for cause and after a hearing, the president can be fired at any time for a good reason, a bad reason, or no reason. Not only is he subject to the whims of board members; his position can be made untenable by a simple vote of "no confidence" by the faculty or by the persistent clamoring of students for his resignation. This insecurity is not new to our times; it has a long history. Harvard's first president not only was fired but was also personally denounced by Cotton Mather, who called him "a blade who marvelously deceived the expectations of good men concerning him; for he was one fitter to be a master of a Bridewell than a College: and though his avarice was notorious enough to get the name of a Philargyrius fixed upon him yet his cruelty was more scandalous than his avarice." [22] President Tappan was fired by the University of Michigan in 1863 for placing too much emphasis on pure scholarship. When George Stoddard was fired from the presidency of the University of Illinois in 1953, campus wits said the real reason for his removal was that he had been exposed by the local American Legion post as a member of a conspiracy to turn the institution into another Harvard. When Clark Kerr was fired from the presidency of the University of California in 1967 it was apparent that the persistent attacks of students from the radical left, plus the failure of the faculty to support him at the right time, had made Kerr vulnerable to the attacks of politicians from the radical right, however confusing such an explanation may seem. Some presidents are fired for moving too fast, others for moving too slowly; some for being too imaginative, others for lacking imagination; some for being too vigorous, others for lacking vigor. And for every one who is publicly fired there are many who are eased out in a genteel manner or are persuaded to accept early retirement. Whatever else it may be, the presidency is not a secure haven.

In spite of the insecurity, presidency of a college has great attractions for a man who likes to play a conspicuous role on an illuminated stage while engaged in tasks of undeniable social significance. Whether his talents are great or minor, a president is never obscure. He presides at commencements and at a wide variety of other ceremonial functions. Off campus, he is in great demand as a public speaker—the nonacademic public would always rather hear from a president than a professor even when the professor knows more about the subject under discussion. He is interviewed by the press and on television and is invited to serve on committees and commissions. He is the honored guest at social events. When he becomes president his name is automatically listed in *Who's Who in America* regardless of his success in office. And eventually some building on the campus will bear his name.

The president is always the best source of publicity for a college. No matter how many public relations officers are employed, it is the president who can command the attention of the press when news releases are ignored. Many of the prestige colleges first came to public attention when they had presidents who had strong views and expressed them vigorously. A president who is a good manager and nothing more can hold a college together for a time, but it takes one who is also a bold intellectual leader to make a weak college strong and bring its strength to the attention of the public. Unfortunately, the necessary combination of talents is all too rare.

14.   The Power Structure of Academic Institutions

A university is an enormously complex institution consisting of students, faculty, administrators, alumni, a board of regents or trustees, and a vast array of supporting personnel—secretaries, clerks, accountants, and maintenance people. A college is less complex, but it too includes all these basic components, although in smaller numbers. It would be optimistic to expect that such an assortment of individuals—who cannot agree even on the goals of the institution—would work together without frequent conflicts which must be resolved. Someone must be in charge; someone, or some group, must have the authority to decide.

To an outsider—and to many of the protesting students—it appears that authority rests with the president, who has, to be sure, all the symbols of power. If his is a major university, he sits in a spacious paneled office with a fireplace and has secretaries and assistants on call. He lives in a mansion provided by the university and rides to work in a chauffeured limousine. He administers a multimillion-dollar budget, appoints vice-presidents and deans, makes speeches, and meets the press.

But when an industrial leader, statesman, or admiral moves into a university presidency he quickly discovers how little real power is inherent in his new office. If his requests, suggestions, orders, and edicts run counter to the wishes of faculty or alumni, the academic tradition, or the tribal customs of undergraduates, they are likely to be ignored and there is little he can do about it.

If he tries to replace a tenured professor with a better one the entire faculty will band against him. If he tries to alter the customs of social fraternities—if he urges them to practice the brotherhood they preach or suggests that they ought to act like civilized human beings during "hell week"—he will be viciously attacked and it is doubtful that his own board will support him. If he attempts to reduce the football team to an amateur status he will be denounced by sports writers as un-American and hanged in effigy by his students. The faculty will sympathize but will secretly be happy to have their president so deeply involved in a nonacademic controversy that he has no time to trouble himself about academic matters.

University administration differs from other kinds of administration because of the president's peculiar relationship to other members of the organization. Students are not employees. And faculty members are employees only in the strictly legal sense that every good professor quite cheerfully ignores. By a tradition that dates from the Middle Ages the faculty is the policy-making body. But the faculty of a contemporary American college or university shares its responsibility for policy with a board of trustees or regents that in most cases holds the final legal authority. The fact that a president stands between these two policy-making bodies, each of which wants more power at the expense of the other, makes his task more difficult than that of the head of an industrial, governmental, or military organization in which power flows from the top downward. In a university power flows in all directions. Sometimes it seems not to flow at all.

The fact that university administrators must face enormous responsibilities with only limited authority is inherent in the nature of academic institutions. The obligation of a university to push back the frontiers of knowledges requires that both students and faculty members be free to inquire, to challenge, and to examine critically all the assumptions and beliefs society holds most dear. Inevitably, a strong academic institution will harbor individuals who hold divergent and unpopular views. An institution of higher learning ceases to be effective when the administrator attempts to exert the kinds of control considered normal in a non-academic institution of similar size and complexity.

Veblen saw no need for administrators. His solution was simple: "All that is required is the abolition of the academic executive and the governing board. Anything short of this heroic remedy is bound to fail. . . ." [23] Veblen was well aware that with the disappearance of the administrative structure the university, as a complex organization of undergraduate, graduate, and professional schools with their titles, ranks, credits, and degrees, would fall apart. And he wanted it that way.

Frustrated by administrative decisions that have gone against them, professors sometimes share Veblen's dream of a university without a president or deans and are fond of pointing to the medieval university as a model. Protesting students at Berkeley and elsewhere, supported by Paul Goodman, have insisted that university presidents are good for nothing except keeping the sidewalks clean.

Obviously these are merely aggressive reactions to frustration. No one who surveys the problems calmly can really believe that a contemporary American university can operate without an administrative structure of some sort if it is to pay faculty salaries, provide buildings and equipment, and keep the records that are essential if degrees are to be granted to students. If all the administrative problems were turned over to faculty committees, the chairmen of those committees would become administrators no matter what they were called, and would have little time for teaching or research. If they failed to exercise their authority the institution would become a shambles. If they did exercise it they would be no less vulnerable to student and faculty criticism than the present administrators. The animosity now directed toward presidents and deans would be turned upon them. Soon they would demand higher pay to compensate them for their additional responsibilities. And if all administrative responsibilities were assigned to students, who could rarely remain in office long enough to gain an understanding of the complex problems and who at best are immature, the results would be chaotic. The faculty would resign en masse.

If students are to have time to learn and faculty members are to be free to teach and to engage in their scholarly pursuits, the university must have an administrative structure. And if the university is to be better than fifth-rate the man at the top of that structure—the president—must do much more than keep the sidewalks clean; he must exert moral and intellectual leadership over the entire academic community. Though an established institution can survive for a time under a president who is nothing more than a manager, American universities have made their greatest forward strides when they had strong presidents. Harvard under Eliot, Hopkins under Gilman, Chicago under Harper, Clark under Hall, Michigan under Angel, and Stanford under Jordan provided the models and set the tone for higher education while universities with weak presidents fell behind. It is difficult to name a university president in office today who ranks in prestige or influence with those of the past; it may be that the role of the president is changing and that decision-making must now be more widely distributed. This is the view of Clark Kerr, who holds that the president of a contemporary university must be primarily a mediator. But other presidents disagree. President Perkins of Cornell says that if the president is not in charge he ought to be, and adds ". . . the role of the university president as bashful educational leader is mostly nonsense and greatly overplayed." As for letting students run the university, Perkins says, ". . . the student is a student. He is at the university to learn, not to manage; to reflect, not to decide; to observe, not to coerce."

It seems probable that most university presidents, while agreeing with Perkins in principle, will continue in practice to play the role of mediator recommended by Kerr. The firm and decisive role is both difficult and hazardous. It can succeed only when the president is a man of great talent, broad perspective, and high prestige who has both the faculty and the board firmly behind him; otherwise it can lead to disaster, as it has over the years in a number of universities. On the other hand, it must be admitted that the mediators have not recently had great success in dealing with student and faculty rebellion.

The primary responsibility of the board of regents is to act as a buffer between the university and the community at large on which it relies for support. A good board interprets the public will to the faculty and students but represents the academic community when it speaks to the outside public. Without such a buffer the faculty would be much more vulnerable to attack than it now is—most board members spend far more time defending the institution, its faculty and its students, than the faculty is ever aware.

Veblen contended that the universities of his day were dominated by businessmen who gained access to boards of regents by providing the money and then selected business-minded presidents to carry out their instructions. This thesis may have come close to the facts of some private universities of 1900 or 1910 when men who had made their millions in steel, oil, or railroads were providing the major support for Stanford, Chicago, or other newly established universities, but it does not fit so neatly today. Many of our major universities, including those termed private, now receive major portions of their funds from public sources, and none is obligated to a single millionaire for its support. Today's boards of regents represent many facets of American life: politics, the professions, and even organized labor as well as the business community. And most of the men and women on today's boards are themselves well educated. Frequently their view of higher education is far more comprehensive than that of many academic men whose concern is with only a single discipline. It is the exceptional board member who has an ax to grind or who is narrow, bigoted, ignorant, or cantankerous who provides that basis for the stereotype held by many professors. Most boards are neither as ignorant nor as powerful as professors believe. Moreover, they have lost some of their power during the past half-century while faculties have gained in power. The Board of Regents of the University of California, for example, has discovered that it cannot ignore the Academic Senate of that institution, which is a very powerful body. It cannot ignore the students either. Much the same thing can be said of other major universities. The Harvard faculty does not take orders from the

Harvard Board of Overseers, nor does the faculty of any first-rate college or university take orders from its board. Unfortunately, many faculties do not yet understand the nature of their own power and some have used it badly.

Policy, in America's great universities, as well as in the better colleges, both public and private, is not made by any single body —it results from the interaction of countervailing forces. The board reflects the public conscience and acts as a buffer between the institutions and the larger community. The faculty, through its elected representatives—a faculty senate, council, or committees—has the primary responsibility for academic policy. It decides what kinds of students may be admitted, what courses and curricula shall be offered, and what the standards of graduation shall be. The administration sets the tone for the institution; calls attention to problems and suggests solutions; announces, carries out, and interprets policy; and interprets the decisions of the board to the faculty and the decisions of the faculty to the board.

This leaves the students; what part do they play in policy-making? Thirty years ago—even ten years ago—the answer might have been "Not very much." Their major protests were against unsuccessful coaches (who were routinely hanged in effigy), dormitory regulations (which were universally held to be too restrictive), and faculty control of the student press. On only a few campuses did the students of an earlier day express concern for educational quality, for the competence of the faculty, or for the content of the curriculum. But now all this is changing. And because it is changing, boards, administrators, and faculties must now decide how much responsibility they will give to undergraduates. They will find the decisions painful because the student demands, if accepted, will upset the entire power structure of the university. If students are to have more power, all the other elements will have less.

When their demands bring students into conflict with administrative authority, the faculty often sides with the students, for professors tend to share the students' distrust of administrators.

But when students demand changes in academic policy or control over it, when they ask for better teaching and less emphasis on research, or when they protest the dismissal or denial of promotion to a popular teacher as they have done in a number of institutions, they come into direct conflict with the faculty. It is the research-oriented faculty rather than the administration that is primarily responsible for the neglect of undergraduates. It is the faculty that is responsible for the rigorous standards that cause half of our students to drop out before graduation. And on all but the most backward campuses, the decisions about which professors shall be retained and promoted are made by faculty committees rather than central administration. The board merely affirms the decisions already made.

What responsibilities for policy-making may properly be delegated to or shared by the students? And what kinds of power and responsibilities do they really want? The answer differs from one institution to another, but it seems clear that the demands of some of the more politically active students are far more modest. William Peterson, Professor of Sociology at Berkeley, after denying that free speech was the real issue in the Berkeley rebellion, asked "If not free speech, what then is the issue?" and he answered ". . . preposterous as this may seem, the real issue is the seizure of power." [24] Peterson quotes a former student's open letter to undergraduates calling on them to "begin an open, fierce, and thoroughgoing revolution on this campus. . . . Go to the top. Make your demands to the Regents. If they refuse to give you an audience, start a program of agitation, petitioning, rallies, etc. in which the final result will be CIVIL DISOBEDIENCE. . . . ORGANIZE AND SPLIT THIS CAMPUS WIDE OPEN." And another student said belligerently: "We'll see who runs this university!"

On most campuses, however, even the more extreme student leaders are asking for something less than complete control of the university. Most students are willing to settle for three things: freedom from the parietal rules of the university governing student behavior both on and off campus; the right to express their opinions about the competence of individual faculty members with the clear understanding that these opinions will have a significant influence on the decisions made regarding faculty promotion and tenure; and the right to participate as voting members of the faculty committees that construct the curriculum.

The subject of parietal rules was discussed in an earlier chapter. While most faculty members probably will be happy to give up whatever responsibility they now have for student behavior outside class, they are likely to be much more reluctant to allow students to judge their teaching competence or to play any substantial role in deciding what shall be taught and what courses shall be required for a degree.

The practice of letting students judge the value of courses and the competence of teachers, though far from universal, is by no means new. Many colleges have made provision for student polls on these subjects for thirty years or more. Even in colleges in which such polls are not officially conducted, many individual faculty members distribute questionnaires to their own students asking the student to indicate weaknesses in the course and to make suggestions for its improvement.

After using such questionnaires in my own classes for nearly thirty years I am thoroughly convinced that students, whether they are freshmen, seniors, or graduates, can make sound judgments and offer many useful suggestions to any teacher willing to ask their opinions. They know when a course is badly organized and when the teacher is dealing with subjects that are of little interest to him. They can tell when he has made careful preparation for his class and when he comes to class unprepared. And they can distinguish between popularity and professional competence. Most of the voluminous research on the subject of student ratings of faculty members confirms these judgments.

But whether student rating may properly be used as a basis for decisions regarding faculty tenure and promotions remains a subject of hot debate on many campuses. Faculty members who oppose such use contend that students cannot possibly judge the teacher's competence as a scholar and cannot reasonably be expected to know when he is teaching them facts that are not true or principles that are unsound or outmoded. They contend that the students are likely to be overimpressed by youth, vigor, and a colorful personality and to underrate wisdom and depth of understanding. An additional difficulty is that teaching is only one of the professor's responsibilities and students cannot possibly judge the professor's competence as a faculty member or a research scholar.

The strongest justification for the use of student ratings is that no one except the students has any real knowledge of a teacher's effectiveness in the classroom. By long academic tradition, deans and senior faculty members visit the classes of junior members only when specifically invited. Even if the department head should visit a class once or twice he would have much less basis for judging the entire course than a student who is in class every day. If students are not asked to rate the faculty, teaching competence is likely to be ignored when the instructor comes up for promotion or tenure, with the result that some who are totally incompetent as teachers will become permanent members of the faculty.

It seems probable that the compromise solution, now in practice in a number of colleges, will be extended to others. Students will rate all their teachers and these ratings will be available to the faculty committees and administrative officers who make decisions regarding tenure and promotion. But those who make the decisions will also give consideration to other aspects of the instructor's competence, including his scholarly productivity and his contribution to the college as a member of the faculty. It is not likely that the final decisions will ever be delegated to students except in a very few institutions.

Student demands for a larger voice in curriculum-making are likely to lead to a similar compromise. The views of students should be heard and will be heard. Students will be asked to form advisory committees to recommend curricular changes and in some institutions students will become voting members of curriculum committees. In many cases the students can identify defects of which the faculty is unaware. It is not likely, however, that the faculties of more than a few institutions will surrender complete control of the curriculum to the students.

Though a college or university should provide open channels of communication to allow students to express their views on all matters of legitimate concern to them, a faculty would be most unwise to transfer to undergraduates the responsibility for basic academic policy or for determining the long-range goals of the institution. Such decisions require a vast array of scholarly information, long years of experience, and maturity of judgment. Given time, a bright student can, of course, acquire the information, gain the experience, and achieve the maturity. But by the time he has done so, he will no longer be a student. He will be a professor or, if fate is unkind, a university president.

PART FOUR
PROBLEMS AND
PROPOSALS

15. Problems for Long-range Planners

Who and How Many Should Go to College?

No educational institution that is open to everyone can properly be called "higher." All colleges require evidence of previous education, usually in the form of a high school diploma, and many require further evidence of educational achievement and academic promise in the form of superior high school grades plus high scores on college entrance examinations. They also attempt, by means of references from high school counselors, to find evidence of high motivation, intellectual curiosity, and maturity. But most colleges do not discriminate on the basis of sex, and most of those responsible for selecting students now agree that it is not legitimate to discriminate on the basis of race or religion. Though there are persistent rumors of hidden quotas for minority groups, most college officials deny that such quotas exist. I can say with confidence that in the state institutions with which I am most familiar there are no quotas—academic aptitude is the only criterion used.

Colleges select students on the basis of high school grades and entrance test scores because both have been found to correlate with college grades and because the combination provides a better prediction than either one alone. School grades predict college grades because the traits and habits that enable a student to do well in high school are likely to persist when he enters college. Any student of good native intelligence, particularly if he has the advantage of a stimulating home background, can make good grades by working hard, reading what he is told to read, carrying out assignments on time, and giving on examinations the kinds of answers teachers prefer. Entrance examinations give a better indication of intellectual capacity because they are scored against national norms while high school grades differ from one school to another.

But the use of these criteria in selecting students is open to a number of criticisms. Both criteria tend to discriminate against students from culturally deprived homes in which there is a lack of intellectual stimulation, inadequate opportunity to learn good English, and few books or magazines, even when the student has high native intelligence and great potential for adult achievement. The use of high school grades discriminates in favor of girls and against boys because girls, being more mature and more willing to do what the teacher expects, make substantially higher grades in high school than boys—about three-fourths of all high school valedictorians are girls. The entrance examinations measure academic intelligence and knowledge but they do not measure, and are not in most cases designed to measure, persistence, motivation or creativity.

But the most serious and legitimate criticism is that these criteria predict only college grades. Since everyone agrees that getting high grades is not the proper reason for going to college, and since the correlation between grades and adult achievement, though positive, does not appear to be very high, it seems entirely possible that our "most selective colleges" are not admitting the ones who would profit most from a college education. It may be that some of those who make high grades in school and college will, after graduation, rest back contentedly with the smug assumption that anyone with a degree from a good college has it made, while some of those denied admission might have profited much more from the same education. This is a fear that haunts all conscientious entrance examiners.

Entrance standards in a selective college ought to be based upon predictions of what a student is likely to achieve with a college education that he could not have achieved without it. The question should be not "What kinds of grades will he make in college?" but "To what extent is it likely that a college education will enable him to make a greater contribution to society twenty, thirty, or forty years after graduation?"

To say that it is difficult to answer such a question does not mean that it is impossible. Finding the answer will require a long-range study of individuals whose traits and capacities are carefully assessed before they enter college and for whom records are kept for thirty or forty years after graduation, until they have had full opportunity to demonstrate their capacity for leadership and their greatness or mediocrity as adults. A special effort should be made to discover future leaders who do not fit into the conventional mold and who consequently do not make the kind of high school records that will admit them to selective colleges. Psychologists should have started such a study fifty years ago—it should not be delayed longer. It will require a multimillion-dollar research grant but it will yield results of far greater consequence than most of the grants now being handed out by foundations and the federal government. We shall probably discover that many of the individuals now enrolled in the most prestigious colleges ought not to be there, while a considerable number of those now denied admission should have been granted full scholarships. Having made this discovery, we can make better use of the available educational facilities and resources.

The present rigorous entrance standards have not been in effect long enough to enable us to say whether the students now admitted will achieve greatly as adults. The fact that they do well in graduate school proves only that academic skills carry over from one academic level to the next. We do know that Harvard did not restrict its entering class to academically talented students at the time when Franklin Roosevelt was in college and that it was much less selective when John F. Kennedy was a freshman than it is now. And it cannot be said that the most selective colleges have demonstrated their ability to select a large percentage of the individuals who will find their way to high political office, even though it ought to be obvious that those who are to rule the nation should have the best possible education. Half of our present U.S. Senators and state governors attended state colleges or state universities, while many of the others attended church-related colleges that do not have rigorous entrance standards.

The fact that most of those who have won the Nobel Prize in science have been individuals who made good grades in school and went on for their Ph.D.s, while several of those who have won the same prize in literature were school or college dropouts, suggests that colleges have not yet learned how to identify or provide for creative people. Why, one wonders, were Hemingway and Faulkner not offered scholarships to the selective colleges? To say that genius does not require formal education is a lame excuse.

Each year during the decade of the seventies approximately four million young Americans will reach the age of eighteen. As a nation we must decide how many of these should be afforded an opportunity for higher education. Though at least three-fourths will graduate from high school and some colleges will admit all high school graduates, it would be optimistic to assume that so large a number can profit substantially from higher education. Some of them could not survive to graduation because while high schools graduate students who have made only a straight D average, most colleges drop any student who cannot make a C average during his freshman year, and Cs are much harder to make in college than in high school.

Some would answer the question of numbers on the basis of the need for college graduates by government, industry, and the professions, a demand that has grown with the years and will continue to grow. However, many educators support the view that the need for higher education should be justified not by manpower demands but by the need for educated citizens regardless of their vocations. They have proposed that the liberal portion of a college should be available to all who can profit from it. And some are convinced that, with proper adaptation of the curriculum to individual differences and with improved elementary and secondary education, some kind of liberal education at the college level could be made appropriate for nearly all.

Others sharply disagree. Many academic men, as well as many of those outside of academic institutions, are convinced that too many young people are in college already. They doubt that more than a small proportion of college-age adolescents are or can become qualified for any kind of learning properly described as "higher." Howard Mumford Jones expressed the view of many university professors when he said "University education is a privilege for the competent, not a right to be claimed by the many." [25] But just *how* competent must a student be to profit from a college education? What kinds of competence does he need? And do the present entrance standards really give evidence of that kind of competence?

At present most community junior colleges and about half the state and church-related colleges will admit almost any high school graduate who applies, though they advise some against entering. But other state and denominational institutions admit only the upper half, upper third, or upper 10 per cent of the high school graduating class. Some of the most selective institutions require candidates to be within the upper 2 or 3 per cent of the age group in academic talent. Obviously these various practices reflect widely different answers to the question "Who ought to be admitted to college?"

My own guess is that perhaps a third to a half of all high school graduates can profit enough from some kind of higher education to justify the time and expense, while still others need vocational training after high school. I do not share the optimism of those who would send everyone to college. The first requirement should be a positive desire for higher education—a desire on the part of the student rather than his parents.

Whatever our opinions may be, two facts seem clear enough. The proportion of young people who can profit substantially from higher education is much larger than it was thought to be by our grandfathers at a time when only 2 or 3 per cent went to college and most of these came from the upper socioeconomic classes. And the number going to college is now, and will continue to be, much higher than the number proposed by those who look upon higher education as something appropriate for only the favored few.

Who Should Pay for Higher Education?

In societies in which the opportunity for education is restricted to those whose parents can pay for it there can be little vertical mobility. The upper classes will be well educated; the peasants will remain illiterate. The lines between the social classes will be rigid. Consequently a nation such as ours, which is committed to equality of opportunity and which accepts upward social mobility as desirable, must provide free schooling for all. And this must include schooling at the highest levels.

We are a long way from achieving our goal of equal opportunity. Even today the child whose parents are affluent and well-educated has a far better chance of getting a good education than a child of equal native intelligence who comes from a poor family. The scholarships available in the private colleges provide for only a very small proportion of the students who need them.

Even in the publicly supported colleges, higher education is by no means "free." The student who goes to college instead of getting a job immediately after high school sacrifices most of the $12,000 to $20,000 he might have earned had he been employed during those years, and many families cannot afford such a sacrifice. If he attends a residential state college he pays from $1000 to $1500 a year—$4000 to $6000 for the four undergraduate years—for board, room, clothing, books, travel, and incidentals. In addition to this, most state colleges charge "fees" of $200 to $300 a year and many of them charge some part of the tuition cost to students.

To prosperous families who are able to send their sons and daughters to private schools, these costs may seem low, but to the average American family, which has an annual income of no more than $7000 or $8000 even in these affluent times, they are prohibitive. Students from most of the 75 per cent of American families that have incomes of less than $10,000 a year can attend even state colleges only if they earn money to pay part of the cost themselves. It is reasonable, and may be educationally advantageous, for them to work during the summer and for a few hours each week during the school year to earn money to help defray their living expenses. But college today is hard work in itself and the assignments require a great deal of time. If students must work additional hours to pay a part of the tuition cost, many will be excluded who ought not to be excluded. It follows, I think, that no part of the cost of instruction in a state college should be charged to the students.

If the American dream of equal opportunity for all young people is ever to be achieved—and we still are a long way from achieving it—the availability of higher education must be totally unrelated to the economic level of the student's parents. In an affluent society, higher education as well as elementary and secondary education should be provided for those judged most likely to profit from it and to make a greater contribution to society as a result of it. Once the students have been selected on this basis, the state or the nation should be prepared to underwrite the cost and to look upon it as a necessary investment in the nation's future.

Although a number of cities support universities, and the federal government provides some assistance, most of the cost of public higher education is provided by the various states, each of which maintains one or more colleges or universities. But because of the increased mobility of the American people, a good case can be made for more federal and less state support. To cite a personal example, I was educated at the expense of the taxpayers of Ohio where I attended public schools, a state college, and the state university. As soon as I received my Ph.D. degree I left Ohio, never to return. Should the cost of my education have been assessed to the taxpayers of Ohio, to those of Washington where I now live, or shared by those of California and New York, in which I have worked? It seems obvious that some sort of federal support for my education would have been more appropriate. And my case is not exceptional. Three-fourths of the 300 faculty members in my present college were educated outside the state of Washington—the state that gets the benefits of their education. Since some of our states export many college graduates, while others import many graduates from other states, a larger amount of federal assistance would seem to be the only way of distributing the cost fairly to all who are likely to profit from it.

Because good higher education is expensive, the cost will be high. But I think most Americans will now agree that the education provided at public expense should be in no way inferior to that available to students whose parents are able to pay the cost of private college education. This conviction is most firmly rooted in the West, where good private colleges are fewer, but is growing even in New York and New England. Until the public colleges are made as good as the best private ones, equality of opportunity is little more than a myth. And as a nation, we can afford the cost without hardship to anyone. The world's greatest university could be built at a cost no greater than that of landing one man on the moon.

What's in a Name?

The statistics of higher education are hopelessly confused by the fact that there is no agreement as to how higher institutions should be classified. The confusion is compounded by the upward mobility of American institutions of higher learning—over the years academies, vocational schools, and normal schools have become colleges, colleges have become universities, and universities have become multiversities. But even the word *university* has no clear meaning in this country. Of the 300 institutions that carry that word in their titles, 45 are single-purpose undergraduate colleges offering no degree beyond the baccalaureate, while many of the others do not offer the academic doctorate or have no schools of law, theology, or medicine.

If *university* is defined as a comprehensive institution that accepts responsibility for the advancement of all the major areas of higher learning; that offers a graduate program leading to the Ph.D.; and that offers courses in preparation for the practice of medicine, law, and other learned professions, then not more than 85 institutions in the United States can qualify. Some of these have only borderline qualifications—only 40 have been able to gain admission to the prestigious Association of American Universities. But there is not the slightest chance of restricting the use of the word *university* to these few institutions that follow the traditional European pattern. The many private and church-related colleges now called universities are not likely to give up the title. Many others will surely demand it.

A large and growing number of our higher institutions fall into a category for which we have not an appropriate name. Though they lack some of the essential features of the traditional university they are far too large and complex to be called simply *colleges*—a word usually applied either to a single-purpose undergraduate school or to a graduate or professional school within a university. Most of these in-between institutions enroll from 3000 to 10,000 students, though a few are much larger. Some had their origins as private or church-related colleges located in an urban setting; in response to the increasing demand for higher education, they have added new programs and accepted more students. Others are state institutions that had their origin as agricultural or teachers' colleges but now have added liberal arts programs and programs leading to the master's degree. In either case they have, in recent years, added many new buildings, expanded their library and laboratory facilities, and upgraded their faculties. In many cases their annual operating budgets are from three or four million to ten or fifteen million dollars. Because they now include several different colleges, each with its own dean, their administrative structure resembles that of a university more than that of a single-purpose college.

Most of the nonpublic institutions within this category already have changed their names to "university." State colleges find the change more difficult because it requires action of the state legislature. In several states the change has been opposed by a local land-grant university that has only recently escaped the "cow college" label and shudders at the thought of letting the one-time teachers' colleges become competing universities.

Despite such opposition, the expanded state colleges in Ohio, Michigan, Indiana, Illinois, Arizona, and several other states have succeeded in changing their names. Others, such as those in New York, have become campuses of state university systems—a move likely to cause them to lose their separate identity, their individuality, and their freedom to innovate.

Critics charge that the change in name often comes before the change in fact. It would be more accurate to say that it usually comes when the institution is something more than a single college but less than a university. Those who defend the change of title say it helps the college develop into the kind of institution it ought to be. They point out that both students and faculty members are status-seekers who have somehow gotten the notion that to be a "university professor" or a "university student" is more prestigious than to be a "college professor" or a "college student." However unfounded such an assumption may be, it is clearly true that the students are gravitating toward the universities. And young instructors with newly acquired Ph.D.s seem much more willing to accept employment in something called a university than in a college even when the pay is the same.

College officials say that by changing the name of the institution they not only can attract better faculties but will be in better position to get research grants from foundations and the federal government. "Why not do it?" they ask; and since the words *college* and *university* have lost much of their distinguishing meanings there can be no very good answer.

It may be that when still more institutions are called universities the larger and more complex universities will seek some still more grandiose title for themselves: multiversity, cosmoversity, or state university system. But those who have a sophisticated knowledge of higher education will not judge institutions by their names, for they will know that some of the best education is found in small ones that remain content to call themselves colleges.

A Confusion of Degrees

American institutions of higher learning now grant more than 1600 different degrees: doctor's, master's, bachelor's, and associate. And though a degree originally was a title, rank, or distinction conferred upon an individual as a mark of proficiency in scholarship, many of the newer degrees, including those in city planning, beauty culture, diesel engineering, petroleum marketing, and police administration, are primarily evidence of vocational training. Whenever a new vocation is added to the long list for which college education is considered necessary, each of several universities thinks up a new degree to top the period of preparation.

In many cases the same initials are used to designate different specialties.* [26, 27] The letters B.S.L. after a name may mean Bachelor of Sacred Literature, Bachelor of Science in Languages, Bachelor of Science in Law, or Bachelor of Science in Linguistics. If the degree is B.S.M the S.M. may mean Sacred Music or Science of Music. The S.S. in B.S.S. may mean Sanitary Science, Secretarial Science, or Social Science. And if the degree is M.S.M.E., the last two letters may mean Mechanical Engineering, Mining Engineering, or Music Education.

The highest degree, as well as the oldest, is the doctor's, which has been conferred by European universities since the middle of the twelfth century—both the University of Bologna and the University of Paris have been given credit by different medievalists for conferring the first. The word *doctor*, from the Latin *docere*, originally meant teacher; the degree indicated that the individual upon whom it was conferred was qualified to instruct

* For much of the factual data in this section I am indebted to Walter Crosby Eells, author of *Degrees in Education* (Washington, D.C.: Center for Applied Research in Education, Inc., 1963) and to Walter Crosby Eells and Harold Haswell, *Academic Degrees* (Washington, D.C.: USOE, 1960).

students. But in the United States, during the colonial period and through the nineteenth century, academic doctorates were so rare that many Americans never met a "doctor" who was not a physician. Many physicians, innocent of history, came to believe that they and only they were qualified for the title, and that any doctor who was not an M.D. was a fraud. Even today, particularly in rural America, anyone who allows himself to be addressed as Doctor risks being called out in the middle of the night on an obstetrical case. And the newer dictionaries, which base their definitions on current usage rather than etymology or history, now give *physician* as the first definition of the word.

The master's degree, which also dates from the Middle Ages, originally was almost interchangeable with the doctor's and continued to be the top degree granted by English universities until after World War I. On the Continent the master's degree became more common in the faculties of arts, while the doctor's degree was used by the professional faculties of theology, law, and medicine. But during the nineteenth century the doctor of philosophy degree became firmly established in German universities as the top degree for all branches of academic scholarship.

The bachelor's degree came into use later than the others and at first indicated not the completion of a course but acceptance as a student in a course of study leading to the higher degrees. Later it disappeared from most of the continental universities but came to be widely used at Oxford and Cambridge and later in the United States.

Though bachelor's degrees are granted indiscriminately to men and women, single and married, this was not always the case. In the nineteenth century some of the colleges for women, because they thought it unseemly to call a woman a "bachelor," granted such degrees as Mistress of Arts or Sister of Arts. But the feminist movement put a stop to that.

The associate's degree, which is granted by many American junior colleges upon the completion of two years of academic work, has been awarded to an estimated half-million students since the beginning of the junior college movement about 1900.

This degree originated in Europe, however, and was conferred by the University of Durham, England, as early as 1873.

In the United States the bachelor's degree has come to represent four years of academic work beyond high school. The master's is granted upon the completion of an additional year (sometimes two) of study of a more specialized nature. The granting of the academic doctorate is based more upon evidence of scholarly achievement in the form of written and oral examinations and a dissertation than upon years of study, but most students pursuing the Ph.D. spend at least three years in graduate school and many spend much more than that.

The more common or standard degrees—B.A., M.A., and Ph.D.—have lost much of their original meaning. Though the A in the first and second degrees refers to the liberal arts, not one graduate in a dozen can even name the seven liberal arts of the medieval university. The master's degree often represents a level of technical proficiency rather than a level of scholarship. And though a Doctor of Philosophy has studied something in depth he may be totally ignorant of philosophy.

Perhaps it is inevitable that the meaning of the words *doctor, master,* and *bachelor* should change with the centuries, but it is not inevitable that we allow the proliferation of new degrees to continue. A degree ought to have a clear meaning that will be understood by everyone.

The present confusion results from our lack of centralized control over higher education; it is one of the prices colleges pay for their independence. No individual and no office has the authority to bring order out of the present chaos by fiat. But the various institutions, through their accrediting agencies, could reverse the trend toward proliferation of degrees and eventually might be able to establish a more orderly pattern.

Proposal

The present confusion could be substantially reduced if colleges would agree to grant only one baccalaureate—the A.B.—

and would let that degree stand for liberal education *and nothing
else*. If this degree were granted when the student has completed
his liberal studies and is ready for specialization or professional
training, many students would receive it after no more than three
years of college work. Professions should require at least the master's degree; for trades and skills that do not require a background of liberal education a certificate or diploma is more appropriate than a degree.

The master's should be the first professional degree. By short-
ening the program leading to the A.B. to three years, the program of specialization leading to the master's could be extended
to two years without increasing the total amount of time required. Much of the specialization now included in the undergraduate major could be provided better by the graduate school
than by an undergraduate college. The master's is the appropriate
degree for teaching, architecture, engineering, social work, and
other professions that require a substantial amount of liberal education before specialization.

The doctor's degree should always stand for a very high level
of scholarly or professional competence. It should not be granted
in narrow specialties or in technical fields that do not require a
theoretical base. The Ph.D. should be granted for scholarly attainment, as it is now, but those scholars who wish to become
teachers should be differentiated in some way from those who are
interested only in research. Those who plan to teach undergraduates in a liberal arts college should have a preparation at
least as broad as the subjects they will be called upon to teach,
plus some sort of a teaching internship.

Doctorates ought to be granted as the first professional degree
in law and theology as well as in medicine. The bachelor's degree
is inappropriate as preparation for the practice of law because all
attorneys should first be liberally educated and then well
grounded in jurisprudence at a level comparable to that required
for the other learned professions. The doctorate in education is
appropriate for those who wish to be intellectual leaders in education, but for school administrators who look upon their task as

primarily managerial, the M. Ed. is more appropriate than the doctorate.

Reforms such as these will come slowly, but it is time to begin. If a few prestigious universities would take the lead, others would follow. And if the accrediting agencies would express strong disapproval of the current proliferation of new degrees, the effect would be salutary.

The Prospect of Declining Enrollments

College officials, because they are still preoccupied with the problems of growth resulting from the high birthrate of the fifties, are not yet giving much attention to a fact that seems certain to cause them much distress in the 1980s. During the late seventies and early eighties the number of Americans in the eighteen-to-twenty-two age range will decline by about 15 per cent. This is not a guess but a fact, or a projection of a fact, for all the babies who will reach college age during those years have been born and counted and neither the immigration figures nor the rate of infant mortality is large enough to affect the figures significantly. The number of live births in the nation fell from a high of 4,308,000 in 1957 to 3,629,000 in 1966, probably the fastest rate of decline in the history of the world.

No one knows whether the decline will continue; prediction of birthrate is so risky a venture that nearly all the forecasts of the past have been erroneous. Textbooks written in the thirties predicted that the low rate of that decade would continue and that the population of the nation would never rise above 150 million. In 1945 demographers rightly predicted that the rate would rise after the war, but they wrongly predicted that the rate would decline to the 1936 level after just a few years: the high rate continued for fifteen years.

Today many demographers predict another upswing when the postwar babies themselves become old enough to be parents. Since 20 million girls were born during the fifties compared to fewer than 15 million in the forties, we can say with certainty

that the number of women of childbearing age will rise during
the decade of the seventies. But it is possible that the drop in the
number of births per potential mothers will be so great as to offset that fact. The fertility rate of births per thousand women
aged fifteen through forty-four declined from 122.7 in 1957 to 90
in 1966 and continues to fall. It would not need to go very much
lower to keep the number of births well below the 1957 high
even though there are now more potential parents.

Many conflicting theories have been advanced to account for
the rise and fall of birthrates. In the twenties the declining rate
was attributed to prosperity—it was pointed out that the rate was
low in all the more advanced and prosperous nations. But in the
fifties the *high* birthrate was attributed to prosperity—it was said
that parents had more children because they could afford more.
Obviously these were guesses rather than statements of proved
fact.

One thing seems certain. Parents who know how to control
birth and have no religious objection to doing so will have large
families only when they want them. And wanting them or not
has some of the characteristics of a fad or fashion. In the fifties it
was fashionable for young American parents to want many children as quickly as possible. Today it seems more fashionable to
postpone childbearing and to plan smaller families.

Though the decline began before the pill was available, it is obvious that the pill has made control more effective. Its extended
availability, combined with the apparent decrease in desire for
large families, seems likely to result in a continued decline in the
number of births per family. And if the "morning-after" pill
should become available, a still sharper decline seems certain.

Whatever the causes, and whether or not the decline continues,
the decrease in the number of children already born in the sixties
offers both opportunities and threats for educators. In the elementary and secondary schools it will bring an end to the teacher
shortage and an end to the boom in school-building construction.
Teachers can be selected more carefully, the available money will
go farther, and if it is used wisely the result can be better education.

The decline in college enrollments may be smaller than the 15 per cent decline in births because of a steadily increasing proportion of the age group going to college. This is by no means certain because it is possible that the proportion going to college may have reached a plateau by 1980. It cannot exceed the proportion graduating from high school and seems certain to stop well short of that.

Let us suppose that the rising percentage of the age group that goes to college does partially offset the decline in total numbers so that the decline in college enrollments is no more than 10 per cent. What will be the effect on our institutions of higher education?

Though to some it may not mean a great deal, for others it will be disastrous. The stronger and more prestigious institutions, which now reject many applicants, will maintain their present enrollments by lowering entrance standards slightly. But if half our colleges are able to do this and thus keep their enrollments stable during a period when the total number of candidates is declining by 10 per cent, it is obvious that the other half—the weaker and less prestigious colleges—will face enrollment declines averaging 20 per cent. And this will occur within a time span of only six or seven years.

The colleges hardest hit will be those that rely on student tuition fees for a substantial part of their budgets. It will be necessary for such colleges immediately to reduce the size of the faculty. They will be unable to employ new instructors or to replace those who leave or retire. If the decline continues over a period of years the college will be left with a faculty of old men, mostly in the upper ranks.

Colleges that depend on tax support rather than on tuition fees will not be hit quite so soon or quite so hard. But when the state legislature next considers the biennial budget the amount provided will surely be reduced. Eventually the effect on the structure of the faculty will be much the same as in the private colleges. And both public and private institutions that have amortized the building of dormitories out of student rental fees will face a financial crisis.

The decline in undergraduate enrollments will come at a time when graduate-school enrollments—which will not be affected until later—are reaching an all-time high. It has been predicted that from 30,000 to 45,000 Ph.D. degrees will be granted annually in the early eighties. Of the half of the recipients who have hoped to become college or university professors, many will find no positions available. Perhaps the federal government and industry will be able to absorb those who have specialized in the natural and social sciences, though this is by no means certain. It is unlikely that there will be any large demand, outside educational fields, for those with doctorates in the humanities. Many of them will find it necessary to seek positions in junior colleges or high schools where they will be faced with the problem of meeting certification requirements.

If there should be even a mild depression in the early eighties, many men and women with master's and doctor's degrees may find themselves on the unemployed list, just as many were in the thirties. If prosperity continues it seems likely that most of them can be absorbed into the economy in one way or another, though many will not get the kinds of jobs they want. At best it is likely to be a painful period for academic men. If I were a young man I would take care to get a tenured position in a financially stable institution before the declining birthrate reaches the colleges.

The colleges hardest hit will be those that charge high tuition rates without being able to demonstrate that they offer superior educational quality. When the competition becomes acute they will be unable to attract enough students to justify their continued existence. It will not be surprising if some two or three hundred of them fail to survive.

On the plus side is the fact that when enrollments cease to grow there will be less need for new buildings, consequently a larger part of the budget can be used for salaries. And since a larger proportion of the nation's population will be in the twenty-five-through-sixty-five age range, it should be easier for taxpayers to support public colleges without undue strain. Students will no longer find it necessary to scramble so frantically to be admitted to college and the surplus of candidates for instructorships will make it possible for colleges to select their teachers more carefully, giving attention to the special personality traits that make the difference between competence and incompetence among teachers who are equally intelligent and well educated. And perhaps colleges will be able to demand that the graduate schools give more attention to the problem of providing an education appropriate for those who are to teach undergraduates in liberal arts colleges.

16.   The Conventional Wisdom of Academia

If a perceptive observer from another land were to take a close look at all the colleges and universities in the United States he might reasonably conclude that the higher learning in America rests upon the following set of assumptions:

1. That the unit of learning called a college education begins with grade 13 and must require four years of nine months each.

2. That a school year properly runs from late September until early June.

3. That a student should enter college in his eighteenth year regardless of whether his rate of maturation has been fast or slow.

4. That the best way for a student to learn is to sit in class for sixteen hours each week throughout his undergraduate years.

5. That educational achievement is best measured in units called "semester hours," each of which represents class attendance of fifty minutes per week for eighteen weeks—or by quarter or trimester hours that can be translated into semester hours.

6. That a baccalaureate degree should be granted upon the accumulation of about 126 of these units, properly distributed as to subjects, with an average grade of C. And, since C is supposed to mean average, that students who fall below the average should not graduate.

7. That grades should be based in substantial part on written exercises called "examinations." And that a student taking an

examination must never be allowed to consult his notes, use reference materials, or communicate with anyone—he must rely on sheer memory.

8. That during all his class hours the student should be instructed by someone called a professor, instructor, lecturer, or teaching assistant.

9. That the ideal preparation for a faculty member is the program that leads to the Ph.D. degree.

10. That professors will be more effective teachers if they devote a considerable portion of their time to activities that, though widely varied in nature, all are called research. And that only those who are engaged in research can be called productive scholars.

11. That the teaching of highly specialized courses to older students is more difficult, or at any rate more praiseworthy, than teaching courses of a broader and more liberal nature to freshmen and sophomores, and that consequently such teaching should be the privilege of higher-ranking and better-paid faculty members.

12. That every student is, or ought to be, an apprentice scholar who has come to college in order that he may learn the techniques and traditions of scholarship by sitting at the feet of mature scholars who are "productive."

13. That because of a recent cataclysm called "the explosion of knowledge," college professors and the courses they teach must now be very narrowly specialized—anyone whose interests are not highly specialized does not deserve to be called a scholar and should be denied access to the higher academic ranks.

Our visitor might also conclude that the most highly selective and prestigious colleges base their programs and entrance requirements on these further assumptions:

1. That a college in a position to be highly selective should give preference to those students who are judged most likely to make high grades in college.

2. That higher education of high quality is possible only to students who fall within the upper 10, 5, or 2 per cent of the age group in academic potential as measured by high school grades and College Board scores.

3. That a student whose academic talents place him within these upper ranges should be segregated during the college years from students of lower potential—that he should be enrolled in a special "prestige" college where he will have little opportunity to associate, socially or academically, with students who did not make similarly high grades in high school or who made lower scores on the College Board examinations.

Though all these assumptions have been challenged, they remain the basis for the standard practices in the great majority of our higher institutions. The visitor, knowing that academic men place great emphasis on the importance of verifiable evidence from research, might reasonably ask to see the research data that support such assumptions. But he would discover that such evidence does not exist. Most of the standard practices reflect tradition and not much else.

There is no evidence to support the assumption that a "college education" must take four years rather than a longer or shorter period of time—the choice of four years is little more than a historical accident. There is ample evidence that any unit of learning should take longer for some individuals than for others. The academic year of nine months is a relic of an agrarian society in which boys were needed for work on the farm during the summer months. More recently it has been defended on the ground that study is difficult during hot weather but there is no real justification for it in an urban society that has air conditioning.

The practice of admitting students to college at the age of eighteen was established in the late nineteenth century when the four-year public high school was superimposed upon an eight-year "elementary" school and colleges began to require the high school diploma of entering freshmen. Until that time many students who had attended Latin grammar schools or other preparatory schools entered college at fifteen, sixteen, or seventeen. The practice of sending girls through school at the same rate as boys ignores the well-established facts of differential rates of maturation in the two sexes. It causes girls to be in a class with boys who are less mature than they in everything but chronological age. The result is that girls make consistently better grades in high school than boys—about three-fourths of the high school valedictorians in the nation are girls, as already noted. Consequently girls find it easier than boys to gain admittance to colleges that select students on the basis of high school grades. If the lower schools were to make proper use of nongraded approaches it would be possible for colleges to admit both sexes at an appropriate level of maturity and to make proper allowances for individual differences in maturation in both sexes. But tradition, plus the strong arm of academic bureaucracy, stands in the way of making the necessary changes.

The assumption that sitting in class is the best way for a student to learn has often been challenged. The practice survives only because no one has yet found a better way of teaching large masses of students. And, though neither students nor professors have much confidence in the counting of semester hours of credit as a measure of educational attainment, it has proved difficult to avoid some kind of academic bookkeeping when students seek degrees and employers demand them.

Though grades have little meaning except as evidence of readiness for more formal education, they too are difficult to eliminate in a society that dotes on symbols of achievement. But the proposed shift from an A–B–C–D–F to a Pass–Fail system would not eliminate the problem; it would merely be a change from a five-point to a two-point grading system that would offer no recognition for achievement above the minimal level. If grades were completely eliminated the degree would be nothing more than a certificate of attendance; indeed, it would not even be that—most colleges no longer require class attendance.

The practice of basing grades on examinations during which the student is denied the use of notes and reference materials is totally unrealistic and indefensible. It is based upon the implied assumption that memory for facts is all-important. It is not a good preparation for adult life—professors and other adults writing reports, articles, or books are expected to discuss their work with others, make use of all available reference materials, and take whatever time is necessary for writing and rewriting. Even a newspaper reporter who must meet an early deadline is expected to consult references to get his facts straight and he would be considered incompetent if he did not make full use of his notes. Only in schools is the use of reference materials and notes called "cheating." If colleges would substitute more realistic tasks for the present examinations, the problem of cheating would disappear except for the occasional case of outright plagiarism that would not be too difficult to detect.

The practice of assigning the most broadly comprehensive liberal arts courses to teaching assistants while senior professors teach more specialized courses is a direct result of making the liberal arts college an appendage of the graduate school in which the stress is more properly on specialized research. This practice is less common in the smaller and independent liberal arts colleges.

The examination of some of the other assumptions I have listed raises complicated issues that deserve more detailed exploration.

The Myth of the Apprentice Scholar

Veblen held that a university ought to be a community of scholars to which students who are apprentice scholars come in order to learn the traditions and procedures of scholarship by sitting at the feet of mature scholars. He shared the view of Helmholtz that "every student should add at least one brick to the ever growing temple of knowledge." The many university professors who take the same view of the purpose of the higher learning tend to teach their courses—even those enrolling freshmen and sophomores—as though every student intended to become a scholar in the professor's discipline. History courses are planned as a first step toward the making of future historians, literature courses are taught for future literary scholars, psychology for future psychologists, and mathematics for future mathematicians.

In such courses the majority of undergraduates find little that is of interest to them or relevant to their life plans because only a small percentage of the six million students in college today plan to become productive scholars in the professor's discipline. Most of the students in an undergraduate history course choose the subject not because they wish to become historians but because they want to know what has happened in man's long past and what it all means. They study literature not to become literary critics or scholars but because they hope to find, in the world's great literature, something of relevance to their own lives. They study psychology not to learn the more sophisticated techniques of laboratory experimentation with rats or pigeons but because they hope to learn something about their own behavior or that of their friends. But the scholarly professor who is preoccupied with his own disciplines often fails to give the students what they want, need, and have a right to expect as a part of their liberal education.

Only in the graduate school can it safely be assumed that every student is an apprentice scholar. The teacher of undergraduates ought to accept the fact that many of his students are taking the last course they will ever get in that particular discipline. His job is not to "cover the subject"—he cannot possibly do that—but to select from his discipline those facts, principles, and ideas that are of most value to all those who need a liberal education.

The successful teacher of undergraduates is a scholar who is also a man of broad vision, able to see beyond the boundaries of his own discipline. He searches for meanings and is prepared to examine the problem of values. He sees the relevance of his discipline to other areas of knowledge and to the lives of his students. He asks himself not "How can I make productive scholars of all these students?" but rather "What can I offer them from my discipline that will give richness and meaning to their lives?"

He is prepared to give an honest answer when a student asks "What does it mean to me?" or "Why should a future lawyer, businessman, or housewife be interested in poetry, mathematics, physics, history, or philosophy?" And he knows how to stimulate the interest of students who come to class only because the course is required. The professor who lacks these talents and these skills, and this breadth of vision, however competent he may be as a scholar, is not qualified to teach undergraduates in a liberal arts college.

The Myth of Exploding Knowledge

The currently popular idea that there has been "an explosion of knowledge" in recent years is a dangerous half-truth that leads many professors and students to the utterly false conclusion that broadly liberal education is no longer possible—that all education must be highly specialized and that all courses must be taught by specialists. This dubious bit of logic is used by many academic specialists as a justification for expanding the requirements for undergraduate majors in their own fields at the expense of the more comprehensive liberal courses.

What has been called an explosion of knowledge could more properly be called a sharp increase in the number of scholarly publications and an accelerated output of technical data, particularly in the natural and behavioral sciences. A student in a graduate or professional school can reasonably be expected to be familiar with such data—a medical student, for example, should be reasonably conversant with new developments in medical science. But most of the new data have little meaning to undergraduates until they are digested and interpreted in the broader perspective of other disciplines. The undergraduate needs a synthesis of recent discoveries with older knowledge that is new to him. In my own discipline it seems safe to say that the number of research papers dealing with psychological problems in the past twenty-five years exceeds the total number published in all the previous history of man. The number of publications listed in

Psychological Abstracts increased from 5000 in 1945 to 17,000 in 1965. There has indeed been an explosion of something—perhaps of the number of psychologists competing for degrees and promotions. But if you ask a psychologist "What do you know about the nature of man and his behavior that was not known to anyone a quarter of a century ago?" he will find it difficult to give firm answers that are of much consequence to anyone except other psychologists. Most of the facts and principles that are of significance to the undergraduate who studies psychology as a part of his liberal education—the nature of human motivation, the processes of perception, the processes of personality formation, the nature and extent of individual differences, and the processes of learning including both classical and operant conditioning—were well known to psychologists in 1940. What has been added is new evidence concerning these principles that requires some modest amount of reinterpretation of previously announced conclusions, plus a vast amount of detailed research data the meaning of which is not yet entirely clear.

I am not qualified to comment in detail on the other behavioral and natural sciences, but it seems clear that much of what is called "the new mathematics" and "the new physics" was known to some mathematicians and physicists at least a quarter of a century ago. It has been more than half a century since Einstein made his major contributions.

In the humanities, where knowledge is not cumulative in the same sense it is in the sciences, new ideas emerge still more slowly. It is doubtful that any contemporary dramatist or literary critic has a better understanding of the nature of tragedy than Sophocles had twenty-four centuries ago. It is obvious that the new poetry does not render obsolete that of Lucretius, Dante, or Milton. It is at least debatable whether the approaches used by contemporary philosophers are superior to those of Plato, Aristotle, Aquinas, Descartes, Locke, Hegel, James, or Dewey. Consequently an extreme emphasis on contemporaneity is inappropriate in teaching these subjects.

The transmission of the cultural heritage is still an essential part of the education of civilized men. No amount of new knowledge can ever make this heritage obsolete. Those who do not remember the past, as Santayana has reminded us, are condemned to repeat it. All the dark ages that blot the pages of the history of our own and other civilizations began when the older generation failed—for one reason or another—to transmit the cultural heritage to the young. If students are to understand the culture of which they are a part it is essential that they gain a firm understanding of the literature, art, music, philosophy, and history of both the recent and the more distant past.

During his undergraduate years the student should learn to see the world in the perspective of historic, geologic, and astronomic time. With this background he will be prepared to devote his adult years to a continuing investigation of the contemporary world. He will be aware that although there has been in recent years a rapid accumulation of new data there has been only a modest increase in firm and significant knowledge. And there definitely has been no explosion of wisdom.

The Demand for Specialization

Even if it were agreed that there has been a vast expansion of significant knowledge in recent years, it would not follow that a specialized education is the best preparation for the unknown future faced by today's students. It would surely not follow that early specialization should replace liberal education at the undergraduate level. Colleges and universities that prepare only specialists are discharging only one of their obligations for the education of tomorrow's leaders.

Men who have moved beyond the stage of savagery have always been to some extent specialized in their work. Even in the Late Stone Age some men specialized in making arrowheads. In the earliest known civilizations some men were priests, some were warriors, some were shepherds. In classic Greece some men were philosophers and some were architects while others were stonemasons or farmers. But in every age the truly great men were those who saw the world not through the narrowed eyes of the specialists but in broader perspective. Leonardo, Franklin, Jefferson, and Churchill were competent in some of the specialties that engage the energies of mankind, but their greatness resulted from the fact that they were able to rise above their specialties. Even today the need in the higher positions of leadership—for statesmen, university presidents, editors, foundation officials, and corporation executives at the upper levels—is not for specialists but for men of broader vision. Specialists who are only specialists are not qualified for such positions nor will they be qualified in the future. And the colleges cannot safely deny their responsibility for such leadership if they are to be anything more than technical institutes.

The danger of overspecializing before one has become liberally educated was pointed out nearly a century ago by T. H. Huxley, who said in 1874, "Unless we are led to see that we are citizens and men before anything else, I say it will go very badly indeed with men of science in future generations, and they will run the risk of becoming scientific pedants when they should be men, philosophers, and good citizens." [28]

More recently, in an editorial in *Science*, René Dubos said "A society that blindly accepts the decisions of experts is a sick society. The time has come when we must produce, alongside specialists, another class of scholars and citizens who have broad familiarity with the facts, methods, and objectives of science and thus are capable of making judgments about scientific policies." [29]

In the *Folklore of Management* Clarence B. Randall comments on the problems of specialization from the point of view of industrial management: "this modern passion for the proliferation of specialists, and the subdivision of business into watertight compartments, goes straight to the heart of sound administration. Breadth at the top cannot be built on a foundation of narrowness at the bottom. When death or resignation or retirement removes a responsible officer, his place cannot be filled by trying suddenly to make a generalist out of a specialist. Wise and effective leadership is practiced only by those who have overcome, as far as humanly possible, all limitations of the mind." [30]

Randall also comments on the dangers facing a young career

man who fails to gain a broad intellectual background: "The young man who knows but one subject, even though he has mastered it, takes a frightful risk when he applies for his first job. He may be handcuffing himself into a situation where the future is limited, from which there will be no escape. He may rise rapidly at first, only to hit a ceiling which he cannot pass. Or he may have chosen a specialty that will eventually lose importance because of the changes that come in industry." [31]

Though the need of our society for specialists cannot be denied, their training is not the proper responsibility of the liberal arts college. There will be ample time for specialization in the graduate and professional schools. What the undergraduate needs is not the most recent data, most of which is still undigested, uninterpreted, and in many cases not yet fully verified, but the knowledge and wisdom accumulated over the years and centuries which has led to reasonably firm conclusions that should be a part of the repertory of all educated men. The liberal arts colleges, whether they are parts of universities or independent institutions, should resist the forces that are causing them to turn away from their basic responsibility for making the most of man as man.

17. Who Will Teach the Undergraduates?

The Forgotten Man

The undergraduate is becoming the forgotten man of American higher education. As colleges become universities and as universities expand into multiversities, the student who comes to college for a liberal education receives less and less of the attention of the faculty and commands an ever smaller proportion of the resources of the university. Increasingly the money made available to higher education from foundations, the federal government, and private donors goes to the graduate and professional schools of major universities. Since faculty members are likely to follow the money, the small colleges that stress liberal education find it increasingly difficult to attract well-qualified candidates for faculty positions.

In the private universities that charge high tuition fees the undergraduate often gets less than he pays for because in some of these institutions a substantial part of the tuition money paid by undergraduates is used for the support of the graduate school. This fact cannot easily be documented because of the budgetary practices of complex institutions in which some professors teach both graduates and undergraduates, but I have talked with a number of university presidents who admit privately that they could not possibly support their expensive graduate and professional programs without using a part of the fees paid by freshmen and sophomores who, because they receive a part of their instruction in large lecture sections, can be educated at much lower cost.

Though liberal education has many vocal defenders, words have little effect upon the status system that makes the teaching of broadly liberal undergraduate courses unattractive to academic men. Many of the able students who enter graduate school with the intention of becoming college teachers rather than researchers succumb to the subtle but effective indoctrination of graduate education. By observing the people around them they become convinced that the academic man who prefers to teach broadly liberal introductory courses, and who takes the time required to do it well, is likely to be dealt with harshly when the time comes for promotion. By the time they receive their Ph.D. degrees they have concluded that the way to rise in rank, salary, prestige, and national visibility is to devote one's major energies to research and writing while teaching only a few advanced seminars in specialties closely related to that research.

Yet a considerable number of college professors, including some who are excellent teachers, continue to devote their major energies to teaching. Occasionally the students come to the defense of such teachers with results that make the headlines. When students at Tufts University protested the dismissal of a popular assistant professor in 1964, the episode received nationwide attention and became the subject of numerous editorials decrying the excessive emphasis on research. Many academic men found it difficult to see what the fuss was all about, for the dismissal was based on a charge they understood: "The promise of scholarly publication has not materialized." In plain English, the professor was fired because he had failed to publish a sufficient number of scholarly books or journal articles. Each spring faculty members on hundreds of campuses are dismissed or denied promotion for the same reason and no one ever hears about it. This professor was especially vulnerable because he had published a book outside his field—one not based on scholarly research—and in the eyes of many academic men this is a sin more grave than not publishing at all. As scholars saw it, Tufts received unwelcome publicity only because the man against whom it took action bore a famous name and was the grandson of a President of the United States. But the real issue, oversimplified by the battle cry "Publish or perish," is one of growing concern on many campuses.

Those who defend the requirement of research as a basis for promotion present as their strongest argument the fact that unless a professor publishes, the quality of his work is not open to the critical examination of his peers. So long as we persist in the tradition of not visiting each other's classes it is true that the senior professors, department heads, and deans who make decisions about promotions rarely have much basis for judging the scholarship of junior faculty members as it is demonstrated in their teaching. In theory his publications are judged, or can be judged, by competent scholars not only within the institution but in all parts of the nation and the world. In actual practice the journal articles of obscure academic men rarely are evaluated critically in any form that is of much use to those who must make the decisions about promotion. Many an assistant professor has had the experience of publishing a paper based on a year's research and of receiving no response except two or three letters from old friends plus a nitpicking letter from someone who has discovered a minor factual error or a split infinitive. Only the mature scholar, who has arrived, can expect to have his work evaluated carefully by competent scholars in his field.

It has also been contended that unless a professor publishes he is likely to go stale and lose interest in his subject, but the evidence for this is not very persuasive. It may appear to be true in a graduate school where most competent professors do publish, but in the smaller undergraduate colleges there are many professors who retain their intellectual vitality without resorting to print.

Those who oppose the emphasis on research contend that significant published scholarship must always be the work of a few individuals of exceptional talent and that trivial research of the kind that deals with some minor segment of a discipline, explored in great detail—the kind submitted by many faculty members seeking promotion—is a waste of time and energy. They doubt that the careful investigation of minutiae improves a teacher's competence to teach broadly liberal undergraduate courses as they should be taught.

Many college teachers—probably a majority of those who make careers of undergraduate teaching—share these views. They are convinced that teaching itself is a scholarly activity that requires a great expenditure of mental energy. They believe that energy devoted to research must be subtracted from that available for teaching. And they prefer to teach.

Though some of the professors who hold these views may be rationalizing personal limitations, others clearly are excellent teachers who make a lasting impression on their students. Their views rarely come to public attention because they are not put into print, yet these men and women carry the major load of undergraduate instruction. If they become embittered as a result of being passed over for promotion, the quality of undergraduate education will suffer.

The view that every professor ought to be a "productive scholar" was unknown to American colleges until they began emulating German universities in the late nineteenth century. The great German universities of that day (there were only a few of them) were graduate and professional schools with nothing comparable to our undergraduate colleges. Because there was often only one professorship in each department, the man who aspired to a chair could reasonably be expected to be a distinguished scholar who had made significant original contributions to his field.

Since a university is responsible for the advancement of knowledge as well as for its dissemination, our graduate schools can legitimately make the same demand today. At the graduate level, teaching and research are closely related. But the question of whether research and scholarly publication can legitimately be required of *every* American professor, whether he teaches graduates or undergraduates, remains controversial.

In any case such a requirement cannot possibly be enforced.

American colleges and universities soon will employ a half-million faculty members. If each one writes a scholarly book every five years, publishers will be asked to publish 100,000 such books annually—three or four times the total number of books of all kinds now published each year in the United States. If each college teacher were to write just one short journal article each year—a total of a half-million articles annually—most of them could find no outlet for publication unless the number of journals were increased to many times the present large number. These figures make it obvious that the great majority of those who teach college students are not going to be "productive scholars" if publication is to be the only accepted evidence of scholarship. There are just too many of them.

What Is Scholarship?

Even those who are certain that every professor ought to be a productive scholar find it difficult to agree on a definition of scholarship. To many scientists, scholarship means research or the publications resulting from research, but even the meaning of research differs from one science to another. In physics, chemistry, biology, and some aspects of psychology, research usually means conducting a carefully controlled experiment in a laboratory. But in astronomy, anthropology, sociology, and social psychology, because the subjects cannot be brought into the laboratory, experimentation more often takes the form of making careful observations of events over which the experimenter has no control and then drawing conclusions from the observations, using statistical or other mathematical procedures when appropriate.

In history, literature, and philosophy, scholarship takes a wide variety of forms, some of which are called research even though they are not experimental in the scientific sense. The humanistic scholar is expected to collect his evidence carefully, with due regard to procedures that have been established within his discipline, and is usually expected to avoid personal value judgments in drawing conclusions from the evidence he has accumulated.

The fine arts pose a special problem to faculties who wish to promote professors on the basis of productive scholarship. Many faculties are reluctant to accept a painting, a musical composition, or a book of poems as evidence of scholarship. Consequently one who writes critically *about* art, music, or poetry is likely to be promoted ahead of the individual who achieves a high level of creativity in his field. The "artists in residence" or "poets in residence" found on college campuses usually are not accepted as full-fledged members of the faculty.

Even when the evidence of scholarship takes the form of a printed document it is not easy to get agreement as to which books or journal articles should be accepted as scholarly. Many students seem to believe that to be "scholarly" a paper must be heavily documented—a garland of *Ibids*. They have been indoctrinated with the view that it is scholarly to quote the opinions of others but unscholarly to express opinions of your own. Or, if they are studying science, they are apt to believe that it is scholarly to cite facts but unscholarly to draw conclusions or to make value judgments.

Professors take a more sophisticated view but still find it hard to agree on a definition. Is a textbook a scholarly publication? Is a book review? Is an article in *Daedalus, The Yale Review, The American Scholar*, or *Encounter?* What about an article in *Harper's, Atlantic*, or *Saturday Review?* The usual reply from the academic world is that such publications cannot be accepted as evidence of scholarship—that a scholarly publication must be addressed not to the public at large or even to a highly intelligent segment of the general public but to a narrowly defined group of scholars in a single academic discipline.

The underlying assumption is that scholarly writing requires a precision of language and the use of technological terminology that are unfamiliar to those outside the scholarly discipline. And it is true that when a scholar attempts to explain his meaning without the use of a technical vocabulary, or without the use of statistics or other mathematical formulae, his statement is likely to lose something in precision. Consequently many scholars take pride in the fact that their publications can be read by only a select few. This posture is not limited to scientists; many avantgarde critics write in a language that is meaningless to the general public and they, too, take pride in their unintelligibility. Throughout the academic world, a clear and understandable literary style is referred to scornfully as "journalistic."

The fact remains that some of the greatest books ever written contain little esoteric language and can be read and understood by any intelligent individual who has a modest background of liberal education. One need not be a biologist to read Darwin, a psychologist to read William James, or a philosopher to read Plato, Aristotle, or Locke. It is characteristic of the greatest writers that they can make difficult ideas understandable without the use of technical terminology, esoteric vocabulary, the latest professional jargon, or involved syntax. The fact that many of the "Great Books of the Western World" do not conform to the current academic standards of scholarly writing seems to suggest that there is a level of intellectual discourse that goes beyond and above what is commonly called scholarly writing. And, indeed, I think there is, painful as that fact may be to most academic men.

James' *Principles of Psychology*, which appears on some of the lists of "100 Great Books," was written as a textbook. It contains few footnotes and rarely mentions the research evidence that supports the author's conclusions. If James were an assistant professor at a minor American university today and submitted this book as evidence of his scholarship—it was just about the only thing he had to offer at the age of forty-eight—he would probably be denied promotion while some third-rate pedant who used more footnotes and had done more research would move up the ladder.

If Plato were a graduate student today and submitted his *Republic* as a doctoral dissertation, no graduate committee would even consider it. The philosophy department would deny that it is philosophy. Political scientists would call it fantasy rather than a scholarly treatise. Departments of literature would almost certainly reject it, and professors in all the disciplines would complain about the lack of documentation and Plato's failure to include a survey of the previous literature.

When I have posed this problem to university professors and graduate-school deans most of them have defended the present standards, even to the point of insisting that Plato ought not to be granted a degree and that James should not be promoted on the basis of a textbook. They have made much of the fact that both Plato and James lived in worlds vastly different from ours, and some have expressed a conviction that if they were university professors today both would conform to the contemporary standards. This seems to me most unlikely, for neither James nor Plato was a conformist. James did protest vigorously against the restrictive standards of scholarship that were making themselves felt at Harvard while he was there and he never bothered to take a Ph.D. Plato would surely not conform—if the system beat him down he might join Socrates in drinking the hemlock—he would not surrender. Yet if I were a dean of a liberal arts college I would be delighted to have both James and Plato on my faculty no matter what the graduate schools and the accrediting agencies might say. I can only conclude that there is something seriously wrong with the definition of scholarship currently favored by academic men.

There is need for a broader definition that recognizes not one but many kinds of scholarly productivity. The first is the kind found in doctoral dissertations and in most of the journal articles submitted by instructors when they come up for promotion. This variety usually is restricted to a narrow segment of a discipline, deals with a sharply delimited problem the writer has explored in great depth, and is characterized by a great emphasis on rigor, precision, and detail. It draws conclusions from experimentation or other objective evidence and avoids value judgments. Every statement of fact is meticulously documented. But it places little or no emphasis on clarity or literary style.

This kind of scholarly publication, which conforms to the dictum of Helmholtz that every student should add a few small bricks to the edifice of scholarship, is the only kind that many of the younger academic men strive for or seem to be aware of. It has proved to be of great value, particularly in the natural sciences, but it surely is not the only kind that can legitimately be called scholarly. And it is not the most important.

A second variety, which is more characteristic of the mature scholar, rests on a broader base. It moves beyond the factual details and searches for meanings. It consists of analysis and interpretation, the exploration and clarification of the larger concepts, the critical evaluation of the work of others, and the proposing of new hypotheses that go beyond the existing data but serve to stimulate the work of other researchers. An outlet for this kind of publication is found in some of the better professional journals, many of the quarterlies, some of the quality magazines of general circulation, as well as in *Science, Daedalus, The Yale Review, The American Scholar,* and other journals that are not restricted to a single discipline. Many great books, including those of Freud, James, Marx, Darwin, Keynes, Toynbee, Spengler, and Einstein, also fall within this category. Any academic man who denies that such books are scholarly (and some do deny it) surely makes himself—and scholarship—seem ridiculous. These are the books that change men's minds and move the world.

While the first kind of scholarship is appropriate for graduate students and young instructors who still lack the breadth of vision and the range of experience essential to interpretation, this second kind is far more appropriate for those who teach the liberal disciplines to undergraduates. Though not many college teachers can hope to rival the writers I have mentioned, all of them can take the work of these scholars for their models. Perhaps each academic man, as a part of his training, should write one Ph.D. dissertation. But one is enough. After that he should move on to a higher level of scholarship.

A third variety of scholarship selects, interprets, and explains data from an academic discipline or disciplines for the benefit of students who do not have time to read everything available in its original form. Textbook writing should not be scorned, for in its best form it requires scholarship of a very high level. Moreover, it is an excellent preparation for the teaching of undergraduates because it requires the writer to become thoroughly familiar with his discipline, to select the significant from among the vast number of scholarly publications that are of little consequence and best ignored, and to write with sufficient clarity to be understandable to students. Moreover, the author of a textbook must become conversant with the full range of topics covered in a course while the preparation of a sharply delimited research paper gives evidence that the author knows only a small segment of the discipline he is expected to teach.

The printed page ought not to be the only acceptable evidence of scholarship. Socrates was only the first of a long line of academic men whose scholarship has taken the form of oral discourse with students instead of writing. Though it may be that few of today's professors are as successful as Socrates, just as few write as well as Plato or Aristotle, oral scholarship of a high level can be found here and there on almost every campus. It should not be ignored, because of all the forms of scholarship this is the one that has the greatest influence on students. The professor who devotes his entire energies to this kind of scholarship, and who achieves a high level of excellence in it, should never be treated as a second-class citizen but should be promoted regularly to the highest ranks, regardless of whether he is also a writer.

Proposal for the Development of a Balanced Liberal Arts Faculty

Although it is legitimate for a graduate school to select and promote faculty members on the basis of research and scholarly publication, an undergraduate college has additional responsibilities that can be discharged only by a faculty possessing a wider variety of talents. Within its faculty there should be some individuals who publish regularly, but there must also be some who can deliver effective lectures, many who can conduct small seminars with skill, and some who work well with individual students.

Though these skills and talents are by no means inconsistent—

it is entirely possible for an individual to be both a great teacher and a great writer—those who recruit faculty members for undergraduate colleges cannot hope to find enough individuals who both teach well and make significant contributions to the scholarly journals. Even if they could be found, most of them would find that the teaching load customary in a small college makes it very difficult for the good teacher who prepares himself properly for his classes to find time to carry on any large amount of research or to publish more than occasionally. Only a graduate school of a major university can afford to allow more than a few faculty members the kind of very light teaching loads that are essential to those who publish regularly.

The goal of a liberal arts college should be not to recruit well-rounded individuals but to achieve a balanced faculty that, as a team, can properly discharge all the obligations of the college. This achievement is possible only if the college offers alternative routes to promotion for all those who demonstrate a high level of competence in any one of the necessary talents.

Each faculty member should be allowed to decide for himself whether he wishes to be judged on the basis of his publications, his teaching, or both. If he chooses to devote a substantial portion of his time to research and writing, his teaching load should be reduced sufficiently to enable him to plan his research carefully and to write well. When he comes up for promotion he should be expected to give evidence not merely that he has published a specified number of papers but also that he has made some significant new discoveries or that he made a substantial contribution to the analysis, interpretation, and criticism of the work of other scholars. His publication should be judged not only by other members of his department but also by scholars in other institutions. Even the smallest liberal arts college should not turn its back on the professor whose scholarly productivity takes the printed form —when he emerges he should be given every opportunity to make the most of his talents without having to move on to a university. His presence on the faculty will provide stimulation to students and to other faculty members. But a small undergraduate college, unless it is very prestigious, cannot hope to attract many such individuals and ought not to try.

Those members who choose to be judged by their teaching— and in the undergraduate college their number must be substantially larger than the first group—should, when they come up for promotion, be expected to give evidence that their teaching is of a superior quality. Such evidence cannot be objective, but must be based upon a distillation of subjective judgments. The judgments should be those of both students and other faculty members. Students should be polled regularly through anonymous questionnaires carefully designed to distinguish the more obvious forms of popularity from true success as a teacher. A number of such questionnaires is now available.

Whenever possible, recent graduates as well as present students should be invited to express their judgments. By the time a faculty member is ready for promotion to full professor, many of his former students will be mature men and women who have been out of college long enough to be able to look back upon their college experience in perspective. They probably know as much as anyone can ever know about which faculty members made a real difference in their lives. Their opinions about the relative merits of the various faculty members should be available to the deans, department heads, or faculty committees who make decisions about promotion.

The young faculty member should also be encouraged to seek the judgments of senior members of the faculty, based upon actual observation of his teaching. If he teaches large lecture sections he should occasionally invite other faculty members to visit his classes and to write comments for the use of the committee on promotions. If he teaches seminars he should invite other faculty members to join him and to share his teaching in order that they may have an opportunity to judge his leadership without making the fact too obvious to students.

No promotion system in any profession or vocation is foolproof. Inevitably mistakes will be made. But the mistakes being made today are much more numerous than they need be because of the long-standing academic tradition that no faculty member ever visits the class of another faculty member. We should discard the tradition.

If the faculty members are allowed to decide for themselves whether they will devote their major energies to teaching or to research, it is inevitable that some departments in each college will find themselves with too many researchers and too few teachers while others will have too many teachers and too few researchers. But over the years this problem can be solved if each department head, in recruiting new members when vacancies occur, takes care to recruit the kind of people who will balance the department. If this policy of allowing faculty members to choose were to become widespread I am convinced that a considerable number of those now in graduate school would be happy to seek jobs in colleges where it would be understood that teaching was to be their major responsibility. I am convinced, too, that many of the present faculty members who really like to teach, and who could do it well if they had the time, publish occasional minor papers based upon half-hearted research only because such publication is a requirement for promotion. They know that their research is of no real consequence and that their journal articles will not be read by enough people to matter. Given a choice, they would publish only when they have something to say. And they would become better teachers if they knew that quality of teaching was to be an important consideration when the time comes for promotion.

Hopefully, a considerable number of the faculty members would choose to be judged on the basis of both teaching and research. Such individuals should be encouraged to submit evidence of talent in both activities. I have not meant to imply that the correlation between teaching and research is negative—I believe it is positive, but not very high. But no one can say with confidence what the correlation is because of the lack of objective measures of quality for *either* teaching or research.

The goal of the liberal arts college—indeed the goal of each academic department within the college—should be to develop a

team of individuals who can discharge all the responsibilities of
the institution or of the department. There need be no pecking
order, no hierarchy of talents, as there now is in colleges in
which promotions are based on publication while quality of
teaching is ignored. A new promotion system that allows each
faculty member to decide for himself what he can do best will
restore the teacher to his proper place on the college faculty and
will make it much easier to attract the kind of teachers we need if
the liberal arts colleges are to survive.

18.   Finding a Place
for Liberal Education

The Education of Free Men

The history of education records a continuing battle between those who would educate for immediate practical ends and those who take a longer view. The first group asks "What can the student do with what he has learned, right now, or as soon as he has graduated?" and if there is no clear and positive answer they would change the curriculum to make it more immediately practical. Those who take the longer view see education as preparation for an expanded life rather than for a vocation. They are concerned both with the development of individuals as good and effective human beings and with assuring the continuity and improvement of our culture. They believe that these two goals are harmonious and can be achieved through the same program of liberal education. They tend to doubt, however, that education of an immediately practical nature or training specifically designed to prepare students for jobs will contribute in any substantial way to the liberal goals of education.

The curricula of most of our undergraduate colleges represent an uneasy compromise of these two views. The academic men who design the curricula recognize a need for breadth of understanding but they know that most students and their parents expect a college education to be a preparation for employment. Some students, of course, are intellectually curious and eager to explore the universe of knowledge, but a larger number prefer to specialize as soon as possible. Some see no need for courses in the humanities while others wish to avoid courses in science and mathematics. Some of those who anticipate careers in business or industry see little need for any kind of liberal education even though they seek the A.B. degree; they are motivated less by the desire for pure knowledge than by a wish to "get ahead in the world." They want the kind of education that will best qualify them for what the world calls success.

But even the undergraduate who sees his college education as a step toward climbing the social and economic ladder faces a dilemma: the kind of education that gives assurance of a place on the first rung of the ladder differs greatly from the kind that will enable him to take later steps on the upper rungs. The employment officer who interviews the graduate seeking his first job is not likely to be greatly interested in the candidate's knowledge of philosophy, history, literature, or the arts. He is more likely to ask "What can you do right now?" A narrowly technical or vocationally oriented education provides the best answer for getting the first job. But twenty years later, when the same man is ready to move up to the higher echelons, his technical training will have become less important than his liberal education. Then the questions will be "Can you make wise decisions?" "Can you think deeply about important things?" "Do you understand the complexities of the modern world in all their ramifications?"

For the man who wants to be a corporation official, a U.S. Senator, a mayor, a governor, a university president, a school superintendent, a foundation executive, or an editor, a broadly liberal education is of far greater consequence than any kind of specialization. It follows that, although this is not its primary goal, a good liberal education may well prove to be the best preparation for getting ahead in the world or even for keeping a satisfactory job in a fast-changing world in which technical expertise is soon outdated. John Dewey once said, "Theory is, in the end, the most practical of all things"—the most practical because it has the broadest applications. The man who has learned just one specialized vocational skill becomes unemployable when that skill is rendered obsolete by social and technological change. But the liberally educated man, because he understands the basic principles that underlie many kinds of employment, can move with the changing times and can adapt himself more easily to new kinds of employment and to new ways of life. Liberal education makes for adaptability. If it does not, it is not truly liberal no matter what degrees it may lead to.

To identify this kind of education the term *liberal* is preferable to the currently popular *general education* because the latter is so vague that it can mean almost anything. Though some educators use it as a synonym for liberal education at the lower-division level, others employ it as a euphemism for soft courses designed for students who cannot comprehend the liberal disciplines. *Liberal education* is a term with 2000 years of tradition behind it. It is the education that liberates men from the bondage of ignorance, prejudice, and provincialism. It enables us to see the world whole and to see ourselves in perspective. It is the education appropriate for free men who must make wise independent decisions—in the home, on the job, in the voting booth, and on the jury panel.

Academic men disagree both about the importance of liberal education and about its proper place in the curriculum. Many professors, including some of those in famous universities, are not themselves liberally educated, whatever the Latin on their diplomas may say. But a substantial minority of academic men are convinced that at least the first two years of college and a part of the time in the junior and senior years should be liberal in nature. It is this minority that has so far kept the liberal studies from being eliminated from the curricula.

The pressures against them are powerful. The many students who would like to bypass the liberal part of a college education in order to get on directly with something more immediately practical have the support not only of some professors and many of their parents but also of most of those who provide the financial support for higher education. It is always much easier to raise money for a medical, engineering, or technical school, or almost any kind of vocational school, than for the support of a liberal arts program. Congress has always shown more enthusiasm for vocational education than for the teaching of the liberal disciplines. Its first big step toward providing federal aid to higher education was the Land Grant College Act of 1861 which made possible the establishment of schools of agriculture and technology. The Smith Hughes Act of 1917 provided assistance to those high schools willing to shift the emphasis to agriculture, home economics, and the mechanical arts. It was another forty years before the Congress showed any interest whatever in the teaching of either such basic subjects as reading, writing, and arithmetic, or in philosophy, literature, and the fine arts. Even today the major portion of the federal assistance provided to schools and colleges goes to those prepared to shift their emphasis toward practical and immediate goals. The title of the National Defense Education Act suggests that those who drafted the bill saw education as a means of strengthening the national defense rather than as a means of achieving the liberal goals of education.

If a proper balance between the two educational goals is to be maintained, liberal education will need all the support it can get from those who see the need for it and comprehend its importance. We can be sure that practical education will be valiantly defended and stressed by legislators, students, parents, and a considerable number of academic men.

Though there has been much controversy about the meaning and content of liberal education, there is no need to prolong the debate endlessly, for there is a considerable amount of agreement among those who have thought deeply about the matter. Throughout the academic community there has been widespread acceptance of a statement made in 1952 by a committee representing the faculties of three universities, Harvard, Princeton and Yale, and three secondary schools, Andover, Exeter, and Lawrenceville. It appears in a volume titled *General Education in School and College:*

> The liberally educated man is articulate, both in speech and writing. He has a feel for language, a respect for clarity and directness of expression, and a knowledge of some language other than his own. He is at home in the world of quantity,

number and measurement. He thinks rationally, logically, objectively, and knows the difference between fact and opinion. When the occasion demands, however, his thought is imaginative and creative rather than logical. He is perceptive, sensitive to form, and affected by beauty. He knows a good deal about the world of nature and the world of man, about the culture of which he is a part, but he is never merely "well informed." He can use what he knows, with judgment and discrimination. He thinks of his business or profession, his family life, and his avocations as parts of a larger whole, parts of a purpose which he has made his own. Whether making a professional or a personal decision, he acts with maturity, balance, and perspective which comes ultimately from his knowledge of other persons, other problems, other times and places. He has convictions, which are reasoned, although he cannot always prove them. He is tolerant about the beliefs of others because he respects sincerity and is not afraid of ideas. He has values, and he can communicate them to others not only by word but by example. His personal standards are high; nothing short of excellence will satisfy him. But service to his society or to his God, not personal satisfaction alone, is the purpose of his excelling. Above all, the liberally-educated man is never a type. He is always a unique person, vivid in his distinction from other similarly educated persons, while sharing with them the traits we have mentioned.[32]

A more recent statement, which has not yet had the attention it deserves, is that of George Stoddard, who in speaking to the American Association of Land-Grant Colleges and State Universities in 1962 proposed that four tests be applied before deciding that an academic program can properly be called liberal:

1. The subject matter is enduring. It must not be ephemeral, trivial, or simply descriptive. There is a search for abstract principles, generatives, and art forms—for all that gives meaning and value to life. How-to-do-it courses cannot meet the test.
2. The subject matter is whole. It cannot be simply a segment

with no beginning and no end. However brief the course, it will start with questions and bring to bear on these questions the wisdom of the ages and of contemporary thinkers. The course may end with more questions, and perhaps with few answers, but it will require the student to think for himself.

3. The student, at the time, approaches the subject matter without reference to technical application. He may like it just as much, for all that, and will work hard at it. It will not take him long to discover that he is achieving a new literacy, as it were, that will brighten his life on many occasions and in all cultures. He will discern, faintly at first, and then with appreciation, an interchange between what he learns at the periphery and what he most needs at the heart-center of a specialized career.

4. Liberal education is a common language. In liberal education we acquire a language that all persons may employ apart from "shop talk." Technical fields should contribute richly to this pool of communicable knowledge. Every informed person has an interest in mathematics, physics, chemistry, geology, astronomy, biology, anthropology, psychology, and sociology, but there must be some principle of selection for the nonspecialist. An advanced subject is not of itself liberal. As we move up in physics, biology, economics, or logic, the subject matter actually becomes less liberal—less communicable to others. There may be less communication even among members of the guild. In other words, liberal education, while based upon the most advanced thinking and creating, is a form of intellectual currency that can be acquired to some degree by every student.[33]

It will be noted that though the first of the statements describes the liberally educated man while Stoddard's statement deals more specifically with program, the two are harmonious. The many descriptions of liberal education found in college catalogues also reflect wide areas of agreement regarding the nature of liberal education. All agree that a liberal education must include much more than a memorization of facts. They agree that such an education must include an exploration of meanings and the relationships among them and give a considerable amount of attention to problems of values. They agree that the student in pursuit of a liberal education should explore the various empirical, rational, and mystical approaches to knowledge and that he should become familiar with both inductive and deductive methods. And they agree that the student should be free to ask questions, including many questions to which no one can offer firm answers, in order that he may discover how much is known and how much remains unknown.

A liberal education, so defined, can be made available in a variety of ways. It may be organized around the traditional academic disciplines or reorganized into larger patterns that cut across the boundaries of the disciplines. It may focus upon historical periods, cultures, or geographic regions. It may be taught by means of a selection of great books or great ideas. The curriculum is less important than the attitudes of students and teachers and the methods of inquiry employed. If the teacher is wise as well as informed he can make a substantial contribution to his students' liberal education in any course—he need not wait for a reorganization of the curriculum. But it is obvious that *liberal education* has a meaning much richer and deeper than merely the list of courses that lead to the liberal arts degree in a conventional college or university.

Liberal education is most effective with students who are intellectually curious, eager to understand the world about them, ready to explore the mysteries of the universe, but not yet ready to focus their entire interests on a single limited goal such as becoming a dentist or getting into graduate school. Since these characteristics are found in many boys and girls long before they reach college it is obvious that liberal education cannot be the responsibility of the college alone.

Broadly speaking, liberal education begins as soon as a child has learned to read and write. Ideally it continues all his life, but in a formal sense it lasts until he enters upon specialized or professional training, often during his third college year. If the programs in the upper elementary grades, the junior and senior high schools, and the first two years of college were planned as a unit or properly articulated, there would be ample time, during those years, for a liberal education far superior to that now available.

But public school teachers and college professors rarely sit down together to plan the program. With rare exceptions, one group of educators plans the intermediate or junior high curriculum, another plans the high school program, while still another plans the college courses. The three groups work from different educational philosophies and often seem almost unaware of each other's existence except that high school planners are greatly concerned about college entrance requirements.

The lack of coordinated planning results in a shocking amount of unnecessary duplication of content and some serious omissions. Students from the better high schools report that some of their freshman courses in college are more elementary than courses in the same subject that they had in high school. Others report that some college professors assume a previous preparation that does not exist.

The choice of subjects to be offered at each of the various levels rests upon tradition and not much else. Tradition says we must teach history, literature, biology, physics, and chemistry in high school but must postpone philosophy, psychology, anthropology, and economics until the college years. There is no logic behind such a decision because there is no evidence that the latter series of subjects is any more difficult than the subjects taught in high school.

Students should be allowed to study philosophy as soon as they begin to ask the philosophical questions "What is reality?" "What is beauty?" "What is truth?" and "How do we know?" Since bright young people ask such questions long before they enter college, they should be encouraged to explore the possible answers while in high school. Long before they enter college, students ask the sort of questions about themselves and their friends that a good psychology course would provide some of the answers for. There is no good reason why any subject in which students are interested should be postponed until the college years. If the necessary kinds of teachers are not available in high school we should start preparing them without delay.

Even if his instruction in high school has been of the highest quality, a student's liberal education ought not to terminate with the twelfth grade. The average eighteen-year-old American will live for another sixty years. During these years the world will change so drastically that unless he has the broad historical perspective of a truly liberal education he is likely to become an outdated old-timer before he reaches middle age. It is not too much to ask that at least three or four of the student's remaining sixty years be devoted to further liberal education before he undertakes the kind of education that will lead to vocational specialization. The student has the time and the nation has, or can develop, the necessary educational resources.

But if the students who go directly from the high schools to the universities are to be given the kind of liberal education they need, some drastic reforms must be made in those universities. Two steps are essential: the undergraduate student bodies in the large universities must be broken up into smaller units of a workable size in which communication between students and faculty is possible. And each of these units must recruit, maintain, and properly reward a separate liberal arts faculty that is willing to accept the liberal education of undergraduates as its primary responsibility. Happily a substantial number of American universities are now beginning to take these two steps, which are a part of the "cluster college" approach.

The Cluster College as a Solution

To many Americans, bigness seems a virtue, rapid growth a sign of progress. Because automobiles can be turned out more economically on the assembly line of a large factory than in a small shop, some have reasoned that education too should cost less and be of higher quality in a large institution than in a small one.

But comparisons of education growth and industrial growth are not valid. Because students are not interchangeable units, education does not lend itself to mass production. Often the cost per student rises as a university grows. Much more serious is the fact that the quality of education, particularly of liberal education, is likely to deteriorate as the multiplying echelons of administrative authority increasingly separate the students from those who make policy regarding their education. This deterioration may be obscured from outsiders by the institution's growing prestige as a research institute and by the greater visibility that comes with size. But the students know.

Administrators are of two minds concerning this problem. Some university presidents continue to boast of the size of their institutions and insist that bigness is no barrier to educational quality. But others have expressed fears that the larger universities are all but ungovernable. Faculties, too, are divided. Research professors welcome the expansion because it makes possible a higher degree of specialization and because the larger universities usually provide better facilities for research. Those who teach in the professional schools are relatively unaffected by the size of the total university because the professional schools themselves remain small. Even in some of the largest universities the medical school enrolls no more than 300 or 400 students. But the professors who are committed to the liberal purposes of education, and who prefer to teach undergraduates, are deeply troubled by the breakdown of communication among members of the various departments and by the increasing alienation of students from the institution that comes with growth.

Many students accept the anonymity of the large campus—perhaps because they have never known any other kind—and some prefer it. Those who want to specialize early in their college careers find the opportunities for specialization greater on the larger campuses. Those who take pride in the football team like to be identified with universities large enough to field teams that can go to the bowl games. Some say they prefer large institutions because of the opportunity to meet more people, although it is doubtful that the typical student at Ohio State, Berkeley, or NYU really gets acquainted with as many people during his college career as does the student in a small college. But a growing number of students on the larger campuses are becoming vigorously critical of the massive bureaucracy, registration by computers that deny the student his opportunity to select his teachers, large lecture sections that make it impossible for a professor to know his students, and administrators who are remote figures known to students only through the daily newspapers. They have charged that the university has become a vast, impersonal machine.

Professors who grow weary of this complaint reply, "If you don't like it here why don't you transfer to a small college?" It is true that many of the nation's 600 colleges that enroll fewer than a thousand students would be glad to accept transfers from a university. Though a few of the more prestigious ones turn students away, many of the small rural parochial colleges find it difficult to attract enough students even in today's market. In these colleges, because there are no graduate students, even the freshmen are taught by full-time faculty members most of whom spend little time on research. They devote their entire energies to teaching—exactly what the students say they want. Dormitories are small and intimate; there is a weekly assembly at which the president speaks to the students; professors and students become well acquainted.

But when university students hear the suggestion that they move to a small college they respond with indignation. The intimacy of a small college is not what they really want. Though they are unaware of it, the fact is that most university students are status-seekers who want to be associated with a "name" institution—that is why they chose a large university in the first place. Even those who reject other middle-class traditions are convinced that a big institution must be better than a small one. They are proud of the fact that the library has a million books, even though they plan to read only a few hundred. They like to boast of the Nobel Prize winners on the faculty even though they are unlikely to meet them. And they could not endure the parietal rules of a small parochial college.

Today's students, however critical they may be of the multi-versity, and however much they may desire a sense of community and an opportunity to work closely with their professors, do not find what they want in an isolated college. Most of them come from urban high schools that are larger and better equipped than many small denominational colleges. They do not share the affection of their ancestors for the elm-shaded campus. They want to be "where the action is" and they are convinced that there is not much action in a small town.

Faculty members too, even those who like to teach undergraduates and who want to work closely with students, are turning their backs on the small colleges. Even when salaries are competitive, young instructors just out of graduate school are reluctant to accept positions in a college with inadequate library and laboratory facilities or with departments so small that they will have little opportunity for association with scholars in their own fields. Faculty members, like students, want the virtues of both small and large institutions without the major faults of either.

Is this an impossible dream? At first it may seem so, but perhaps not. Perhaps we can reorganize our institutions of higher learning so that students in pursuit of a liberal education may enjoy some of the more attractive features of a large campus without giving up all the virtues of a small college.

The idea of breaking up the undergraduate division of large universities into smaller units is by no means new. The colleges within Oxford and Cambridge have been tutorial as well as housing units for centuries. Yale and a few other American universities have made some use of variants of the "house plan" for many years. Forty years ago, Pomona took the first step toward the establishment of what has become the Claremont Colleges, each of which has its own faculty, administration, and student body, but in which both students and faculty members have access to the facilities of the total cluster of institutions located on adjoining campuses.

Since 1960 the development of small undergraduate colleges on large campuses has made rapid progress in some forty universities. Many more are contemplating similar moves. The University of the Pacific was the first to apply the term *cluster colleges* to a group of undergraduate institutions on a single campus and under a common board. The Santa Cruz campus of the University of California was the first state institution to plan a campus from the start as a cluster of colleges. Western Washington State College in Bellingham was the first state college *not* called a university to take steps toward providing small units for its undergraduates. The first of these, Fairhaven College, which is opening in 1968, will enroll 600 students—about 10 per cent of the students in the parent institution. Other colleges will be added as Western Washington expands.

Though the details vary substantially from one institution to another, the basic idea behind all these approaches is to provide, within the framework of the parent university, educational communities small enough to make it possible for students to be treated as individuals and for faculty members to work closely with students. Usually each college has its own separate dormitories, dining facilities, social halls, and recreational facilities that provide the basis for student social life. The fact that the several colleges are within walking distance of each other makes it possible for both students and faculty to make use of the superior facilities of the parent institution. It is possible for each college to have a small basic library in which books are easily found and quickly available, while the university maintains a large research library available to all. Other expensive facilities such as laboratories, auditoriums, and playing fields may be used at different times by the different colleges. This can make for substantial savings in cost because the expensive auditorium in an isolated small college normally is used for only a few hours each week.

A cluster of colleges is not to be confused with a conventional university made up of a graduate school, a school of medicine, a law school, and other professional schools, plus a single large undergraduate college that often has no faculty of its own but must draw its professors from the various departments of the graduate and professional schools. The colleges in the new clusters are undergraduate liberal arts institutions. Each may have a special focus of interest—humanities, the behavioral sciences, or the natural sciences—but each offers a balanced scholarly introduction to the basic areas of human knowledge. Narrow specialization and professional training are reserved for the graduate schools.

Though all cluster colleges stress the importance of small units of students and teachers, there has never been much agreement about the meaning of *small* as applied to colleges. As a rule of thumb it might be said that a small college is one in which each student knows most of his classmates and, by the time he is a senior, is known as an individual by most members of the faculty. Or it may be defined as a college in which the entire student body and faculty can assemble in an auditorium for an occasional convocation where they will have some intellectual experiences in common. The upper limit for such an institution probably is 1000 or 1200 students with a faculty of 60 to 100. Even this may be too large. Many of the institutions planning cluster colleges have limited the size of each unit to 600 students. The new colleges at the University of the Pacific restrict enrollment to 250 each.

The success of the plan will depend in large part on the willingness of the administration and the governing board of the senior institution to give a large measure of independence to the faculty of each college. Each college within a cluster should have its own individuality and be free to develop its own curriculum. Inevitably, the colleges within a cluster will compete with each other and this competition will provide the stimulus for a high level of achievement. But each should be unique and proud of its uniqueness. It may be expected that each student will identify himself not with the university, but with his own college. James L. Jarrett reports a conversation with an English student who was reciting a list of great men. "Oh," said Jarrett, "you're saying that these are all Cambridge men." "Of course Cambridge," the student said with a touch of annoyance, "but more importantly, Trinity."

In the cluster college the policy of faculty recruitment, tenure, and promotion must differ substantially from the policy of the graduate school if the college is to be able to attract and hold the kind of faculty it needs. Though some members of the faculty may choose to hold joint appointments in the college and in the graduate school of the parent university, the central core of the cluster college faculty should consist of scholarly individuals who have chosen to devote a major portion of their energies to teaching undergraduates. I am convinced that there is an ample number of such individuals within our present faculties and that they will make themselves known as soon as it is apparent that the cluster colleges offer them an opportunity to win recognition while engaging in the activities they prefer. At present they keep quiet about their real interests because they know that, under the present policy, an admission that one prefers to teach undergraduates is a barrier to promotion in most universities.

In the smaller units, faculty members and students can work closely together in planning and conducting the educational enterprise. The voices of students will be heard and listened to. The college can again become a true community of scholars in which students, because they are of the community, will feel less need to lash out against the faculty and the administration, and in which good teachers will be respected. If there must be a head man—a dean or a provost—he should be a member of the teaching faculty and a member of the academic community.

Though it seems clear that neither the small isolated college nor the amorphous undergraduate school of a mammoth university can offer today's students what they want and need, it would be a mistake to expect too much of the cluster plan; and it would be a mistake for its proponents to promise more than it can deliver. It is no panacea. It will not solve all the problems facing higher education. Though it makes experimentation and curricular improvement possible, it does not *assure* improvement. It is entirely possible that the professors in some of the cluster colleges may continue to teach the same old things in the same old way.

But the plan does offer a way of restoring a sense of community within the institutions of higher learning. At a time when liberal education is gravely threatened by the emphasis on research, specialization, vocational training, it refocuses the emphasis on undergraduates and on the men and women who teach them and want to teach them. At a time when the status symbols of Academia are rigged against teaching, it again makes the teaching of undergraduates an honored vocation for scholars. If it does no more than that it may well be the most vital innovation in higher education today.

19. Conclusion

The Ideal and the Possible

An author is always tempted to propose an ideal solution to the problem under discussion even though he knows it has little chance of becoming a reality. My ideal solution to the problems of higher education would require a reconstruction of the entire educational system from bottom to top because I am convinced that the American custom of planning each level of education separately lies at the root of many of our problems. I would like to see the development of nongraded elementary and intermediate schools that would make it possible for the brighter, better-motivated, more rapidly maturing students to be prepared for college a year or two earlier than they now are and that would also make it possible for girls, who mature more rapidly than boys, to graduate from high school at a younger age. I would like to remove all vocational training from the high schools and place it in postsecondary vocational schools in order that the high school might provide liberal education for everyone—particularly for the culturally disadvantaged students who have the greatest need of an opportunity to expand their cultural horizons. Under the present system, these are the ones most often advised to take vocational courses throughout their high school years. And I would like to separate the liberal arts college from the university and let the university become what most of the professors really want it to be—a graduate school for professionals and other specialists.

Robert Maynard Hutchins would go even further in the same

direction. He proposes a six-year elementary school, a three-year high school, and a three-year liberal arts college for all, graduation from which would take place at approximately the age of eighteen. Only those interested in and qualified for independent study would be admitted to the university. "The multiversity," says Hutchins, "can do something for graduate and professional students. It can, at least, teach them the tricks of their trade. It can do very little for juniors and seniors, and nothing for freshmen and sophomores. It does no good to exhort multiversity professors to take an interest in undergraduates and at the same time make it clear that appointments and promotions and increases in salary depend on the prosecution and publication of research in which undergraduates take no part. In many multiversity departments an interest in undergraduates is a positively harmful eccentricity, which may be fatal to the prospects of one afflicted with it. For the same reasons liberal education has no chance in the multiversity." [34]

Although I think Hutchins is correct in his assessment, his proposal, like mine for a complete reorganization of our educational system, is little more than a utopian fantasy, representing the ideal rather than the possible. The vested interests that would oppose any such reorganization, supported by the heavy hand of tradition, make so drastic a change most unlikely. And since I do not care to devote all my energies to fighting for lost causes, I shall now propose more realistic solutions.

A Reform Plan for Higher Education

In preceding chapters I have mentioned a number of new programs and procedures that already have substantial support, may now be observed in at least a few institutions, and offer an opportunity for the improvement of higher education. I have also indicated a need for additional reforms. Now I shall attempt to bring the new programs and my own proposals together into an organized pattern that I think has some chance of being accepted and put into operation in many colleges and universities within the next decade or two.

A reform plan must provide suitable times and places for the three aspects of higher education: liberal education, academic specialization, and professional training. It should place the responsibility for each aspect in the hands of faculty members who understand and are deeply committed to it. It must make effective teaching possible at all levels by providing teachers who want to teach at that level and are properly prepared. It must reduce each educational unit to a size that makes it possible for teachers and students to work together in a common cause. The completion of each level or kind of learning should be symbolized by an appropriate degree with a clearly understood meaning. And finally, the reform plan should make higher education of high quality available to all who are properly motivated and qualified to profit substantially from it, regardless of family income level, social background, or race.

All predictions, proposals, and recommendations must make allowance for the number of young people who will want and need higher education in the years ahead. The pressures resulting from the high birthrate of the fifties will continue to plague the colleges for another seven or eight years, but after the mid-seventies those pressures will be substantially reduced, for a time at least, by the sharply declining birthrate between 1957 and 1967. The percentage of those reaching college age who will seek higher education may increase for a few more years, but it cannot increase indefinitely—it will certainly stop far short of the theoretical 100 per cent ceiling. It is probable that by 1980 all the states will provide some kind of postsecondary education or training for all those who want it, as many states do already, but this does not mean that all will go to anything properly called a college. It is more likely that half or more will choose some kind of short vocational courses that are best offered in schools designed especially for the purpose. These courses, which range in length from a few months to a year or two, are not appropriate in colleges or universities that grant degrees. We need barbers, plumbers, machinists, clerks, cooks, and waiters, and we want competent ones, but the training courses required in preparation for these trades do not become a part of the higher learning merely because they are sometimes listed in college catalogues. They belong elsewhere.

No matter how wealthy or how well-educated his parents may be, no student should be admitted to college unless he is eager to engage in intellectual discourse at a high level. Since each student must accept a large measure of responsibility for his own learning, the choice among a college, a vocational school, or no further education should always be made by the student himself. High school counselors should counsel, provide information, and help the student to understand himself; but they should not urge or advise a student to go to college, no matter how high his grades or test scores may be. It is asking a great deal of parents and counselors to let each student make his own decision, but that is exactly what we must ask if college students are to be properly motivated.

Some minimal level of intellectual competence is also necessary for the higher learning. No one can say with confidence what percentage of the population can profit from a college education —the percentage has repeatedly been revised upward over the years—but I feel sure that it is much higher than the number the "highly selective" colleges are willing to admit. In my own classes (in a college that admits most of the upper half of high school graduates) I see many students whose high school grades would have barred them from admittance to Swarthmore or Carleton but who are nevertheless gaining a great deal from a college education. Some of them will go far and may well surpass the achievements of the graduates of more selective colleges. But it does not follow that a high school diploma alone is sufficient evidence that a student is prepared for college. Though the quality of high school instruction has improved substantially in the past decade, the recent campaigns to eliminate "dropouts" have made it difficult for high schools to refuse to graduate any student, no matter how little he has learned. Diplomas from a great many high schools, including some in large cities, are little more than certificates of attendance. Before admitting a student, a college needs better evidence.

Admission to a college, whether public or private, should be based on predictive evidence that an individual is prepared to profit from what the college has to offer and that he is likely to contribute more to society with a higher education than without it. I have little confidence that the usual criteria—high school grades and college entrance examinations—really offer such a prediction with any high degree of validity. We know that these criteria predict college grades, but no one can seriously believe that grades are the reason for going to college. A greater effort should be made, through long-range research that follows students into their adult years, to find better ways of selecting the individuals who will profit most from higher education. We may discover that the student who profits most is not the upper-middle-class son of a professional man who attended the best preparatory schools; it may be instead the bright, culturally handicapped student from an urban or rural slum who made a spotty record in a poor high school but is eager to learn. With the help of a college education, he may eventually become a senator, executive, scientist, civil rights leader, or even the President of the United States. It will be difficult to identify such potential leaders at the age of seventeen or eighteen, but we ought not to let the difficulty overwhelm us—we should try to locate them and see that they get the best possible college education regardless of the grades they made in high school.

Once a student has chosen college in preference to a vocational school and has been admitted to a college, he should be required to engage in an extended program of liberal education before he is allowed to undertake professional training or academic specialization. By liberal education I definitely do not mean the list of courses, with a major and a minor, that leads to the A.B. degree in a conventional college. I mean a program especially designed to broaden the student's horizons and liberate him from the limitations of ignorance, prejudice, and provincialism. Such a program will provide the groundwork not for a single vocation but for a richer life and for a wide variety of future vocations that may not yet exist but in which the student may engage before he retires in about the year 2015. If our colleges and universities are to provide such an education it will be necessary for most of them to redesign their programs. At present an A.B. degree is usually evidence of just a little liberal education plus a great deal of specialization (called "the academic major and supporting courses") and often some vocational training.

To avoid confusion and to put an end to the proliferation of degrees, I have suggested that the A.B. be made to signify liberal education and nothing else, and that no other baccalaureate degrees be offered. The master's is a more appropriate degree for engineers, architects, public school teachers, social workers, and other professionals. The law degree should be either a master's or (better still) a doctor's degree in jurisprudence. Though all these professional degrees should be granted by universities rather than liberal arts colleges, the professional programs should always be built upon an undergraduate program in the liberal arts.

By removing all professional specialization from the undergraduate program it would be possible to grant the A.B. degree after three years instead of four and still provide twice as much time for the truly liberal studies as is now available in colleges requiring highly specialized majors and offering professional training.

Many students in colleges operating under the quarter or trimester plans already take their degree in three calendar years. The undergraduate program could be shortened to three *academic* years without causing undue distress to academic bookkeepers or the accrediting agencies. Colleges could continue to require the present number of semester hours while granting more credit for independent study during summer vacations, on the basis of examinations without class attendance. Credit could also be given for advance placement work done in the many high schools that now offer some college-level work for their brighter students. But a better solution would be to transfer a substantial part of the work now required for the undergraduate major to the graduate schools that are better staffed to offer a variety of specialized courses in each discipline. Since the student would enter graduate school a year earlier, he could specialize for two years before receiving an academic master's, and his program of specialization would be planned by a single faculty instead of partly by an undergraduate faculty and partly by a graduate one. It does not seem likely that this change would be opposed by graduate-school professors—I have the impression that most of them would prefer to teach their own specialized courses if they were given the necessary facilities. Even when a student comes to graduate school with a large amount of undergraduate credit in his major discipline, the graduate faculty often requires him to repeat some of his courses because of a lack of confidence in the undergraduate instruction.

Each profession could decide for itself whether the professional master's degree, built upon a three-year undergraduate course, should require one year of work or two. The program for high school teachers, leading to the Master of Arts in Teaching degree, probably should require two years, half the time to be spent in graduate-level courses in the disciplines to be taught and half in professional work that would include an internship in the schools. The candidate would be prepared to enter his profession at the same age as now (a large proportion of high school teachers now take a master's degree or a fifth year), and at no greater cost. But all teachers would have spent three years in a liberal arts college, public or private, plus two in a university. Many of the more specialized courses in applied mathematics and applied physics that prospective engineers now take in the liberal arts college should be moved to the graduate school of engineering.

The establishment of a three-year undergraduate program without specialization or professional training would make it possible to shift the responsibility for planning and teaching the program of liberal education to those who believe in it. Under the present arrangement this is impossible. The present four-year program is an uneasy compromise of the demands of academic specialists, the professions, and those who wish to protect and defend liberal education. When there is a conflict over who is to have the most of the student's time, the specialists and profes-

Years beyond high school	PRESENT STRUCTURE OF HIGHER EDUCATION IN THE UNITED STATES

8 — DOCTORATE

7 — Programs leading to the Ph.D. and other academic doctorates. The minimum time required usually is three years beyond the A.B., but the actual elapsed time is usually much longer.

6 — Professional programs of various length in medicine, law, theology, etc.

5 — MASTER'S | Professional programs (usually one year in length) leading to the various professional master's degrees. | Programs leading to the M.A. and other academic master's degrees. | (Some doctoral students bypass the master's) | Sometimes open to students with less than the A.B. degree.

4 — BACCALAUREATE DEGREES
(great variety; some academic, others vocational)

This part of the program consists of specialized, professional, and preprofessional courses, often called a "major" and "minor" or "major and supporting courses." These courses often begin in the freshman or sophomore years and take up an

3 — increasing portion of the student's time as he advances through the undergraduate years.
Most of these courses are taught by academic or professional specialists whose interests are centered in their own disciplines.

2 — This portion of the program consists of general or liberal education. It is confined

1 — largely to the freshman and sophomore years and takes up from one fourth to one third of the student's undergraduate time.

HIGH SCHOOL GRADUATION

Years beyond high school	A REFORM PLAN FOR HIGHER EDUCATION			
8	DOCTORATE	Programs leading to the academic doctorates: Ph.D., Sc.D., Ed.D., etc.		
7				
6			Programs of various length in medicine, law, theology, etc.	
5	MASTER'S	Two-year professional programs leading to the master's degree for elementary and secondary teachers, engineers, journalists,	Programs leading to the M.A. degree in the various academic disciplines.	
4		architects, business executives, etc.		

BACHELOR'S DEGREES (in liberal arts only)

3 — Three years of liberal education, terminating in the A.B. degree, for all college students. This program to be offered in state colleges, cluster colleges within universities, and some of the stronger community colleges, as well as in the independent and church-related institutions now called "liberal arts colleges."

2 — All these programs will include the humanities, fine arts, natural and behavioral sciences, and mathematics, with perhaps a period of major concentration in one of these broad areas but with no major in a single discipline during the undergraduate period. No vocational training in the liberal arts college. Students who want vocational training immediately after high school graduation will go to vocational schools rather than to colleges or universities.

1 — This undergraduate program to be planned and taught by a faculty especially selected for its interest in liberal education, its own background of liberal education, and its competence as teachers. The faculty will not be under the control of the graduate faculty of a university—it will have its own standards for promotion.

HIGH SCHOOL GRADUATION

sionals usually win out. But under the proposed plan the entire undergraduate program would be the responsibility of professors who have a deep concern for liberal education, while the master's degree program would be planned and taught by specialists or members of the profession for which the student is preparing himself.

The three-year undergraduate program could be offered by a wide variety of colleges: independent and church-related colleges, state colleges, some of the stronger community colleges, and the satellite or cluster colleges within the larger institutions. As a transitional step, some of these colleges might offer the A.B. after three years, with the understanding that students planning to go on to graduate school probably would be required to take an additional year of specialized work in a university to complete the equivalent of a major before being admitted as full-fledged graduate students. They would receive their graduate degrees at the same age as they do now. Eventually the university would come to accept the fourth year as a part of the graduate work and would plan accordingly.

The smaller independent and church-related colleges can provide sound liberal education only if they are relieved of the responsibility for departmental specialization and professional training. They cannot offer it as long as they let the graduate and professional schools dictate their curriculum as many now do. The fact that the graduate physics department of X University requires entering students to have fifty semester hours of undergraduate credit in physics plus forty hours in mathematics and twenty hours in chemistry means that there are only eighteen hours left for other subjects. This makes it impossible for the college preparing students for that university to offer a liberal education. And if it cannot, it has no right to grant the liberal arts degree.

If the undergraduate colleges were to accept responsibility for liberal education and nothing else, there would be no need for any one college to offer a wide variety of programs. Though there are many possible approaches to liberal education, the student would choose his program by selecting his college. And although the smaller liberal arts colleges, which have only two or three professors in each department, cannot hope to offer strong majors in a single discipline, they could, as a part of the three-year program, offer broad-area majors in the humanities, the social sciences, or the natural sciences, which would draw upon the resources of several departments. Such majors would be more liberal in nature because they offer a better opportunity to synthesize knowledge.

In the large universities, liberal education cannot thrive until it is made the responsibility of a faculty especially recruited with the needs of undergraduates in mind. But the satellite or cluster-college approach now being used in some forty universities can restore liberal education to its proper place in the undergraduate curriculum *if* each of these smaller units is granted autonomy from the graduate and professional schools, allowed to design its own program, and granted the authority to select and promote its own faculty members.

The three-year undergraduate program would make it possible for universities to offer a much stronger master's degree because they could require two years of graduate work of all students. At present the requirements for the master's differ widely from one institution to another and even from one department to another in the same university. Some departments in some universities require a year of course work plus a scholarly thesis, both oral and written comprehensive examinations, and one or more foreign languages. Other institutions, and some departments in famous private universities, grant the same degree for a year of course work with an average grade of B, without comprehensive examinations of any kind. The degree has been appropriately described as "a bit like a streetwalker—all things to all men (and at different prices)."

Under the proposed plan, the academic master's degree—i.e., the master's in an academic discipline, as distinct from the professional master's degree—would always represent two full years of specialized work with appropriate comprehensive examinations and either a thesis or a scholarly paper. The program would combine a substantial part of the present undergraduate major with work required for the present master's degree.

The changes in program at the undergraduate and master's degree levels would not require any great change in programs leading to the Ph.D. except that fewer students than now would bypass the M.A. Most would first take a two-year master's and then spend two or three additional years in independent study and research, during which they would prepare their dissertations. It would be up to each discipline to decide whether course work would be required after the M.A.

Some additional changes in the Ph.D. program are long overdue. The late Oliver Carmichael, former president of the Carnegie Foundation for the Advancement of Teaching, says: "The graduate faculty is usually the ablest of the university staff, the cost of graduate education is greater than any other except medical education, and the need for its graduates—Ph.D. graduates—is unparalleled. Yet graduate schools are more confused, ineffective, and inconsistent in their practices than any other school or college of the university." [35]

The present requirements for the Ph.D., as they are listed in the graduate school catalogues, are not excessive; but the additional requirements imposed by individual professors acting as advisers to candidates for the degree often delay the granting of the degree unnecessarily. It is not unusual for doctoral candidates in some departments—the humanities are the worst offenders—to be held in vassalage for six, eight, or ten years while they assist professors with their research, write and rewrite their own dissertations, take additional courses, pay tuition fees, and postpone the day when they will accept the full responsibilities of adult scholars.

Attrition rates are excessive. To be sure, the doctorate is properly very highly selective, but most of the selection ought to be at the time of admission to candidacy rather than afterward. On this subject Carmichael says: "The records show that less than 50 percent of the candidates for the Ph.D. succeed in achieving it,

while 85 to 90 percent of the candidates for the M.D. are successful. Of those who finally achieve the Ph.D., only a minor frac-
tion receive it in three years after the B.A., the time requirement
announced in catalogues. The average lag is roughly seven to
twelve years, depending upon the subject area of the candidate." [36]

One university has hit upon the solution of requiring any candidate who fails to complete his dissertation within a specified
length of time to appear before a graduate committee, accompanied by his faculty adviser, to explain why. If this practice
were more widely adopted, and the laggards and their advisers
were sharply questioned, the elapsed time between the baccalaureate and the doctorate might be substantially reduced.

The language requirement for the doctorate has been a source
of controversy for many years. The problem could easily be
solved by making whatever knowledge of languages is to be demanded a fixed requirement for *admission* to the graduate school
instead of something to be achieved while the student is pursuing
his Ph.D. The student who wants to work for a doctorate but has
failed to gain a competence of foreign languages during his elementary, secondary, or college years, should take time out to
prepare himself in the required languages *before* he begins to
work on his Ph.D. It is unfair to ask him to pay tuition fees to a
graduate school while he is gaining an elementary knowledge of a
foreign language.

Since the mere possession of a Ph.D. offers little assurance of
even minimal competence as a teacher, a sharper differentiation
should be made between programs intended to prepare college
teachers and those designed to prepare researchers only. The future teacher requires not less preparation than the research specialist, but more. Both programs should demand a high level of
scholarship and a familiarity with the methodology of research in
the discipline, but the program for college teachers should also be
designed to prepare competent teachers. A college teacher, in
addition to his knowledge of his discipline and a good background of liberal education, should possess at least a modest de-

gree of familiarity with the history of higher education in America and elsewhere; with the conflicting philosophies of education that lie at the root of many of our current problems; and with the psychology of learning and of individual differences in learning capacity. I would not suggest an extended list of professional courses—just enough to counteract the total ignorance of their profession and of their responsibilities that now handicaps many young instructors and that limits some older academic men throughout their careers. Perhaps an internship in a college, with correlated reading, would be better than formal courses, but something clearly is needed. A generation ago, college students tended to accept bad teaching as one of the normal hazards of the college experience. Today's students are not so complacent. They are demanding, and have a right to demand, better teaching. I hope that they will continue in their demands until the graduate schools accept their responsibility for providing good college teachers.

The total cost of the reform plan would be no more than the present plan—probably it would be less. The financial demands of the undergraduate colleges would be substantially reduced; consequently the plan would make it easier for the poorer independent and church-related colleges to survive. Since the fourth college year would become graduate work, the graduate schools would find it necessary to add to their staffs, which they could do by employing some of the specialists who now teach in undergraduate colleges and who would be happy to move to a university. The total cost of higher education to students, their parents, taxpayers, and other citizens would not be increased. For students who choose not to go beyond the A.B. degree, the cost of a college education would be reduced by one-fourth.

Reprise

In overview it appears, on the surface at least, that the higher learning in America is in a state of robust health. Never has the public's interest in and concern for higher education been so great. The amount of money flowing into our colleges and universities rises steadily. Educational facilities—libraries, laboratories, classroom buildings, and dormitories—have improved greatly since Veblen wrote. Both entrance standards and standards for graduation have risen in spite of the higher number of students in college. It is generally agreed that students are working harder than ever before; C is no longer a gentleman's grade; and academic aptitude has replaced social class as a basis for admission even to Ivy League institutions.

The proportion of young Americans who engage in higher education has increased steadily over the years and continues to increase. Already it is much higher than that of other advanced nations. Except in a few of the eastern states, there is enough room in colleges for all qualified students *if* those students are willing to go where the colleges are, and if they want education rather than prestige. The college-admissions ratrace is largely an artificial phenomenon created by students and their status-seeking parents who have somehow gotten the impression that higher learning is possible only in private colleges or in a few other prestigious "name" institutions with more applicants than they can accept.

Higher education has made it possible for millions of Americans of many races to move up in the world, live better, earn higher incomes, and live more enlightened lives. It has raised the cultural level of the community and of the nation and has done much to combat provincialism.

The attractions of the academic life are increasing. Faculty salaries in the lower echelons are still low, as they are in all salaried professions; but at the top the opportunities for academic men are steadily expanding. The total incomes of the more fortunate and more successful from salaries, consultant fees, and royalties are rising so rapidly that a professor who forsakes the academic life in the hope of making more money elsewhere is likely to regret it. American professors, in contrast to those in Europe, have always tended to feel sorry for themselves, but they find it increasingly difficult to find justification for their complaints.

The great majority of academic men enjoy a high degree of academic freedom. The widespread attention given to the occasional denials of such freedom proves only that such incidents are rare in most colleges and universities. So long as they confine themselves to their areas of professional competence, most American professors are free to investigate freely, to report the results of their investigation, and to teach the truth as it is known in their disciplines.

Higher education is remarkably free of the major sins that beset big business, big government, or big labor. Considering the massive funds involved, there are remarkably few instances of bribery or large-scale corruption in institutions of higher learning. The great majority of academic men, though they are status-seekers, frequently pedantic, sometimes narrow, and only occasionally profound, probably compare favorably with the men in other learned professions in both intellect and integrity.

Big-time intercollegiate athletics and other diversions that alarmed Hutchins thirty years ago are still with us, but the students are losing interest. Football, with its various sideshows —marching bands, cheerleaders, prancing drum majorettes—and its frequent scandals, survives only because the alumni demand entertainment and because the multimillion-dollar stadium must be paid for. But in time this, too, will pass because we are breeding a new generation of alumni.

Today's students are restless, demanding, and uneasy about the state of the world, but they are also perceptive, informed, and sensitive. They are much less likely than those of a generation ago to judge their classmates on the basis of race, creed, or color; and perhaps they are a little less snobbish about social background. Even the social fraternities—those bastions of tradition —are redefining their concept of brotherhood to include at least a few individuals other than WASP.

But the confusion that troubled Hutchins when he wrote his book on the higher learning grows steadily worse. The distinction between a college and a university is even less clear than it was in 1936. A large number of institutions have entered into an in-between status for which neither term is appropriate; they are too large and complex to be called colleges, yet they lack some of the essential features of a university. Many undergraduate colleges—public as well as private—seem unable to decide whether they are liberal arts institutions, professional schools, vocational training institutions, or preparatory schools for some still higher level of education. In their efforts to satisfy everyone they succeed in doing nothing very well.

As a nation we have not yet decided who or how many should be admitted to college. The decisions of individual institutions and of the various states differ greatly. Consequently an individual's opportunity to go to college depends to a large extent on the part of the country in which he lives, unless he can afford to go to a private school or can pay the higher cost of out-of-state tuition in a public institution. Though there is room in some college, somewhere, for any student intellectually qualified for higher education, the dream of equality of educational opportunity for all American youth is still a goal rather than an achievement because of the high cost. As the academic workload increases it becomes increasingly difficult for a student to earn enough while in college to pay his own way. The half of all American families with incomes below $7000 cannot afford the cost of higher education even in a state college. The young American, regardless of his race, who suffers from the handicap of an intellectually inadequate home background finds it difficult to compete in secondary school with classmates whose family background is more conducive to academic achievement, even when his potential intelligence is as high as theirs. Consequently he makes lower grades in high school and is less likely to be offered a college scholarship. As a result the barriers to upward social mobility are becoming more rigid.

The rapid growth and increased popularity of colleges for commuters are causing nearly half of the nation's college students to be denied a substantial part of the social and recreational life that has always been considered an essential part of the college experience. And the practice of living at home with parents and siblings while in college is likely to delay the achievement of full maturity.

Pedantry still is all too common in the halls of Academe. Much that passes for research consists of little more than a meticulous and exhaustive examination of trivial minutiae. Many professors talk about the importance of great ideas and then grade students on the basis of examinations that stress isolated facts. The quality of instruction differs greatly from one classroom to another even in the same institution. Though some excellent teaching can be found in every college, the large universities in particular are all too tolerant of the substantial minority of professors who are totally incompetent as teachers—a tolerance that is the direct result of a promotion system that gives more consideration to publication than to classroom performance and is not likely to disappear so long as the undergraduate college is subordinate to the graduate school.

Although the Ph.D. has become a requirement for promotion to the higher ranks in most colleges, the programs leading to that degree rarely give much attention to development of the special competencies required of teaching unless it can be assumed that anyone who is a research scholar will automatically be a good teacher. Some of our major graduate schools emphatically deny their responsibility for the preparation of teachers for undergraduates—they want all their graduates to find positions in which research will be the major activity. But the assumption we borrowed from the nineteenth-century German universities— that the doctorate indicates preparation for individual scholarly research—becomes increasingly untenable as more and more of these degrees are granted to individuals who have no intention of engaging in research after they have received the degree. And with nearly half a million faculty members employed by our colleges and universities, the assumption that every professor must publish regularly becomes unsupportable—the numbers alone preclude any such possibility. Failure to promote those who can find no outlet for their publications will result in serious morale problems within our faculties.

Whether undergraduate liberal education is best provided within universities or in separate and independent colleges is a question that remains unanswered; but in both colleges and universities the conflict between broadly liberal and narrowly specialized education becomes more acute with the passing years. While professors working within the protective boundaries of their disciplines glibly express the view that ours is a specialized world in which specialized competence is all that counts or is needed, those who look beyond those boundaries to the world outside see many frightening problems that can never be solved by specialists. The solution to the problems of racial and class conflict can be found only by those who have a deep understanding of human values as well as of the facts made available by psychologists, sociologists, anthropologists, economists, and political scientists. Though wars can be waged by specialists, the road to peace will require understandings that bridge the many academic cultures. The problems of overpopulation and of the pollution of our air and water do not fit neatly within any single academic discipline. Any institution that refuses to concern itself with these problems that threaten the welfare, and indeed the very existence, of mankind cannot properly call itself a university, for it has rejected some of the things that matter most.

Our institutions of higher learning have not yet found a solution to the problems presented by a growing minority of intelligent and potentially productive young people who reject the society around them, live parasitic lives, refuse to grow up and accept adult responsibilities, resort to LSD and other escape mechanisms, and yet are so arrogantly confident of the moral superiority of youth that they find it impossible to learn from adults or to accept the leadership of older people. American colleges have always accepted some degree of responsibility for helping talented young people to make the transition from adolescence to adulthood. So long as most adolescents wanted to become adults, were willing to accept adults as their models, and were eager to accept adult responsibilities in order to enjoy the kinds of freedom available only to adults, it was not difficult for educators to guide them through the transition. Adolescent rebellion could be looked upon as a passing phase.

But the years since the end of World War II have seen the emergence of a new teen-age culture that is remote from, and alien to, the adult world. It has its own outlook, music, art forms, and literature as well as its own philosophy and morality. Many students come to college so thoroughly steeped in the exciting subculture that they no longer have any wish to become adults. Academic men must be aware of this subculture but must not be overwhelmed by it or allow it to replace the more responsible and stable culture of the adult world. Youth has no monopoly on virtue, nor is the youth of today free of the sins of prejudice and hypocrisy of which they accuse their elders. But the complaints of these young people against the adult society cannot safely be ignored, for many of their criticisms have at least some element of validity. The task of the colleges and universities is to merge the best elements of the major culture with the best of the youthful subculture.

Those of us who are responsible for guiding the nation's institutions of higher learning must take care that while we bring to students the most recent data from our various disciplines we also transmit the culture that distinguishes us from primitive men; and we must help students become aware that Western culture is only one of many. While we must deal at times with large groups, we must never forget our responsibility for preserving and defending the integrity of the individual. And while we must live in a technological age, we must make sure that our technology serves the human purpose—that it obeys man and does not become his master.

Notes

1. Thorstein Veblen, *The Higher Learning in America* (New York: Viking, 1935), p. 17.
2. Robert Maynard Hutchins, *The Higher Learning in America* (New Haven: Yale University Press, 1936), pp. 59–60.
3. *Ibid.*, pp. 1–2.
4. Gene Hawes, *The New American Guide to Colleges*, 3rd ed. (New York: New American Library, 1966).
5. James Cass and Max Birnbaum, *A Comparative Guide to American Colleges*, 2nd ed. (New York: Harper, 1965).
6. Veblen, *op. cit.*, p. 149.
7. Manning M. Pattillo, Jr., and Donald M. Mackenzie, *Church-Sponsored Higher Education in the United States* (Washington, D.C.: American Council on Education, 1966).
8. William K. Selden, *Accreditation: The Struggle over Standards in Higher Education* (New York: Harper, 1960), pp. 10–11.
9. James A. Perkins, *The University in Transition* (Princeton Press, Princeton University, 1966).
10. J. Martin Klotsche, *The Urban University* (New York: Harper, 1966), p. 89.
11. Frederick Birmingham, *The Ivy League Today* (Crowell, 1961).
12. Nicholas von Hoffman, *The Multiversity* (New York: Holt, Rinehart and Winston, 1966).
13. Robert H. Knapp and Joseph J. Greenbaum, *The Younger American Scholar: His Collegiate Origins* (Middletown, Conn.: The University of Chicago Press and Wesleyan University Press, 1953), p. 5.
14. Allan M. Cartter (ed.), *An Assessment of Quality in Graduate Education* (Washington, D.C.: American Council on Education, 1966).
15. *The Journal of the Association of Deans and Administrators of Student Affairs*, Bulletin No. 2 (April 1967), p. 11.
16. In *The New Statesman;* reprinted in *Atlas* (March 1966), p. 151.
17. Kenneth Keniston, *The Uncommitted: Alienated Youth in American Society* (New York: Dell, 1965).
18. Paul Jacobs and Saul Landau, *The New Radicals: A Report with Documents* (New York: Vintage Books, 1966).

19. Richard Hettlinger, *Living with Sex: the Student's Dilemma* (New York: Seabury Press, 1966), p. 142.
20. Allan Nevins, *The State Universities and Democracy* (Urbana: The University of Illinois Press, 1962).
21. *Salaries in Higher Education 1965–66*, NEA Research Report R2 (1966), p. 36.
22. Von Hoffman, *op. cit.*, p. 159.
23. Veblen, *op. cit.*, p. 176.
24. William Peterson in Seymour Martin Lipset and Sheldon S. Wolin (eds.), *The Berkeley Student Revolt* (New York: Anchor Books, 1965), p. 369.
25. Howard Mumford Jones in the *Atlantic* (November 1965), p. 160.
26. Walter Crosby Eells, *Degrees in Education* (Washington, D.C.: Center for Applied Research in Education, 1963).
27. Walter Crosby Eells and Harold Haswell, *Academic Degrees* (Washington, D.C.: United States Office of Education, 1960).
28. Cyril Bibby, *T. H. Huxley, Humanist and Educator* (New York: Horizon, 1960).
29. René Dubos in *Science* (November 4, 1966), p. 595.
30. Clarence B. Randall, *The Folklore of Management* (New York: Mentor, 1962), p. 63.
31. *Ibid.*, p. 62.
32. *General Education in School and College* (Cambridge, Mass.: Harvard University Press, 1953), pp. 19–20.
33. George D. Stoddard, "A New Design for the College of Liberal Arts and Sciences," in *School and Society*, XC (May 1, 1965).
34. Robert Maynard Hutchins in *New Republic* (April 1, 1967).
35. Oliver C. Carmichael, *Graduate Education* (New York: Harper, 1961), p. 48.
36. *Ibid.*, p. 195.

About the Author

Paul Woodring was born in Delta, Ohio, in 1907. He is a graduate of Bowling Green University and received his Ph.D. degree in psychology from Ohio State University. Since 1939 he has been a member of the faculty of Western Washington State College, where he is now Distinguished Service Professor of the College.

From 1960 to 1966 he was Education Editor of the *Saturday Review*, and has served since 1966 as Editor-at-large. He was for six years a staff member of the Ford Foundation and consultant to the Fund for the Advancement of Education. In addition to many magazine articles on educational problems, he is the author of *Let's Talk Sense about Our Schools, A Fourth of a Nation, American Education Today* (with John Scanlon), *New Directions in Teacher Education,* and *Introduction to American Education.*

3 3312 00007 3817

LA
226
.W73
1968

73-862

Woodring, Paul
The higher learning in America

Asheville-Buncombe Technical Institute
LIBRARY
340 Victoria Road
Asheville, North Carolina 28801